What people are saying . . .

Thank you, Victoria Dorshorn, for not being silent about the critical need for Christians to speak the truth in love to the issues confronting our nation. Built on a solid biblical foundation, *Victory through Voice* is a book "for such a time as this" that every Christian needs to prayerfully study and then consistently apply.

—Marlene Bagnull, Author, Speaker, and Director of Write His Answer Ministries

I anticipated giving Victoria's new book, *Victory through Voice*, a cursory read and then return to it later without time constraints. As I began to read, I was irresistibly drawn to its relevance in an era of cancel culture where silencing our Christian witness is the prime agenda. Instead of a quick read, I couldn't help but set aside my list of priorities for the day and thoroughly immerse myself into a study of this highly-readable handbook exposing Satan's end-times strategy of cancel culture. Here I found well-presented God's instructions to enable us to stand for Christ and righteousness, come what may. The author is obviously a seasoned, perceptive, devout scholar who has done her homework in researching all aspects of this vital topic. I believe this timely book to be a wake-up call for bold witness to a woke-threatened world that has gone off the tracks.

—Leona Choy, Author, Writing Coach, and Executive Editor of Golden Morning Publishing.

Victory through Voice is a thought-provoking book for our times. The author uses examples from Scripture well to lay a foundation of biblical truth and then applies these principles to the present day. Well-written.

—Tracie Heskett, Multi-published Author, Christian and secular education curriculum

In *Victory through Voice*, Victoria Dorshorn urges all Christians to speak the truth in love to a culture that is increasingly dark and hostile. As the world tries to silence believers, Victoria encourages believers to stand firm. She shows the importance of obeying God rather than pleasing men, even when it results in persecution. She exhorts us to be like the first century Christians and to trust God for the victory.

—Anita McKee, Women's Bible Study Leader and Youth Teacher

VICTORY THROUGH VOICE

How to speak truth when
the culture demands silence

VICTORIA DORSHORN

VP

Victory
Publishing

Baldwin City, Kansas

Library of Congress Control Number: 2021912168
ISBN: 978-1-7345393-3-2 (softcover)

This title is also available as an electronic book, available from major outlets.

Scripture marked KJV is taken from *The Holy Bible, King James Version.*

Scripture marked MEV ® is taken from the *Modern English Version.* Copyright © 2014 by Military Bible Association. Used by permission. All rights reserved.

Scripture marked NKJV ® is taken from *The Nelson Study Bible: New King James Version.* Copyright © 1997 by Thomas Nelson, Inc. New King James Version ®. Copyright © 1979, 1980, 1982 by Thomas Nelson, Inc. Used by permission. All rights reserved.

Scripture marked NLT is taken from the *Holy Bible*, New Living Translation, Copyright © 1996, 2004, 2015 by Tyndale House Foundation. Used by permission of Tyndale House Publishers, Inc., Carol Stream, Illinois 60188. All rights reserved.

Scripture marked RSV is taken from the *Revised Standard Version*, Copyright © 1946, 1952, American Bible Society, A. J. Holman Co. Used by permission. All rights reserved.

Scripture marked NASB is taken from the *New American Standard Bible*, Copyright © 1960, 1971, 1977, 1995, 2020 by the Lockman Foundation. All rights reserved.

Copy Editing: Marlene Bagnull

Author Photo: Sarah Reynolds

Cover photo: Motortion Films

Cover design: DesignsDoneNow.com

Book Layout © 2017 BookDesignTemplates.com

Printed in the United States of America

First edition: 10 9 8 7 6 5 4 3 2 1

For my husband, Rick,
whose faith helps anchor me

"*Yours, O LORD, is the greatness,*
the power, the glory,
the victory, and the majesty.
Everything in the heavens and on earth
is yours, O LORD,
and this is your kingdom.
We adore you as the one who is over all things."
—*1 Chronicles 29:11 NLT*

Contents

Acknowledgments 9

Introduction 11

Silence Disguised as Wisdom 13

Commanded to Keep Silent 27

Silenced by Death 39

Silenced by Sin 51

Our Silence Feeds the Darkness 65

Speaking the Truth in Love 79

Love in Response to Bullies 95

Prosperity—Inverted Persecution 109

Should We Expect to be Persecuted? 127

Real Love as Voice 145

Spiritual Fruit as Voice 161

Speaking Foundational Truth 183

Endnotes 199

About the Author 203

Acknowledgments

I thank my husband, without whose love and patience I could not have completed this project. I thank my family, friends, and writing associates for their reassurance along the way.

A special thanks to Marlene Bagnull, who went above and beyond with editing advice, encouragement, and help. She encouraged me each step of the way.

A big thanks to my beta readers, Charles and Anita McKee, whose encouragement kept me on track and pushing ahead.

Also, a special thanks to all who were kind enough to read the book and provide feedback and endorsements, including Leona Choy, Marlene Bagnull, Tracie Heskett, and Anita McKee.

And, of course, I thank the Lord Jesus, who is my inspiration and Light. Without him, I can do nothing. In him, I can do all things.

Truly, when the culture demands our silence and takes drastic measures to silence us, we can look to Jesus for victory. He provides us the voice we need and the words to speak, through the Holy Spirit.

"When they bring you to the . . . rulers, and authorities . . .
the Holy Spirit will teach you at that time
what you should say."
Luke 12:11–12 MEV

"Despite all these things, overwhelming victory is ours
through Christ, who loved us."
Romans 8:37 NLT

Introduction

You will notice headings labeled "Reflect Further" at the end of each chapter. These questions may be answered individually or in groups. To limit the cost of the book, I haven't left space in the text for your answers.

However, it is my hope that completing these exercises will take you deeper into the gospel. May they enrich your spiritual walk with the Lord Jesus. You might purchase a spiral notebook and track your progress in that—much more cost effective than having to purchase a separate workbook. The main thing is that you study the Word so the Holy Spirit can bring it to your mind when it needs to be spoken.

And if you haven't made a commitment to Christ yet, my prayer is that you will before you finish this book.

In any event, may you be enlightened, encouraged, and empowered by our Lord and Savior Jesus Christ, by his Word, and by the Holy Spirit. May God's love envelope you and enable you to love others. And may you experience and enjoy victory through voice as you speak truth in love to a culture that demands silence.

Jesus answered, "I tell you, if these become silent,
the stones will cry out!"
Luke 19:40 NASB

"But you will receive power
when the Holy Spirit comes upon you.
And you will be my witnesses,
telling people about me everywhere. . . ."
Acts 1:8 NLT

CHAPTER 1

Silence Disguised as Wisdom

WHEN I WAS THIRTEEN, babysitting was the only option for a job besides mowing lawns and shoveling snow. So I tried my hand at it briefly. One incident has stuck in my memory. It was, I could say, my finest hour. Followed by shame and guilt.

While babysitting two boys next door, I faced a difficult situation when one of them refused to go to bed. When I realized he was not going to follow my directions, I decided to bribe him. I would tell him a story. A really good story. He agreed.

I proceeded to tell him the story of Jesus. I told him about a God who had created all that is. A God who loved his creation, especially people. But the people went against God and were bad. They wouldn't mind God, and so there was a division between them. God wanted to bring the people back to himself, so he made a plan.

I told him that God sent his Son to be born as a tiny human in a town called Bethlehem. That the baby's name was Jesus, which means Savior. I told him how Jesus grew up and was a very obedient boy. That he respected his parents and loved God his Father. I told him how Jesus grew to manhood and went about preaching good news to the people, healing those who came in faith.

I don't remember how many of the gospel accounts I mentioned in my tale, but he loved it.

Then I told him about Jesus painfully dying on the cross. For us. Because he loves us. And I told him about Jesus being raised from the dead, alive, seen by his disciples, and then taken to heaven in a miraculous way. All so that we could have new life in him, be forgiven of our sins, and be brought back into fellowship with God.

He loved the story. And he promptly went to sleep.

Wow! Success!

Not only did I do my job, but I shared the gospel. I was a bit proud of myself. And particularly happy when the parents came home and were pleased that the kids were asleep.

But it didn't end there. I told my mom about the event. She said I probably shouldn't have told that story because we didn't know what the parents believed. They might not want their children to hear about Jesus.

Huh? Wouldn't everyone want their children to know about Jesus?

I don't fault my mom for her response. She was brought up in a rural area in a time when most people knew the Judeo-Christian heritage. It wasn't sharing the gospel that she felt was wrong, but that denominationally, those neighbors might view it differently.

She impressed upon me that two things should not be discussed in public or with people we hardly know: politics and religion.

Looking for a different answer, I asked my home economics teacher at school. She backed my mom's position. All the way. Even more adamantly. "Never discuss religion with kids you babysit. You might offend the parents."

Fast forward to the next time I babysat those kids. The little boy asked to hear the story again. Oh, my. I would have loved to tell it again. I could see no harm in it. But I had been told . . . .

I refused to tell the story. That's where the shame and guilt come in. To this day I regret that I crumbled so easily in the face of that advice and refused to tell this spiritually hungry child the true story about Jesus Christ, the Son of God, Savior of all who believe. I can only pray that God sent someone else, at some time in this lad's life, to finish the job of leading him to Christ. But my heart still pains me that I didn't repeat the story and satisfy the longing of his little soul to hear the greatest love story in the world, the truth of salvation.

I don't think that our parents and grandparents, members of the greatest generation, the builders, were consciously enforcing privatization. I don't think they even thought of it as "privatizing" or enforcing "freedom from religion," as is the case now. Those were years when wise people didn't rock the boat, didn't share in public those things considered private, and certainly hid any behavior that was outside the accepted norm of Judeo-Christian morality.

I'm not excusing them. I just think they meant well, though the counsel was ill-advised and contrary to Scripture. They were focused on cordial social interaction rather than spreading the gospel. Many of them, no doubt, believed that only ministers were qualified to "preach the gospel." Lay people were to simply sit in pews on Sunday and live good lives the rest of the week. Their lives were their testimony.

People were supposed to see their honesty, excellent work ethic, and fidelity, and recognize that such high standards were the fruit of the Christian faith (or of going to church).

Unfortunately, keeping their faith *private* stifled their witness for Jesus Christ. Christians learned to be silent—and then to compromise. Church members began to consider the gospel only during church hours. Door-to-door witnessing was left to "cults" or fringe movements like JWs and LDSs. Witnessing to strangers was "out of line."

As a result, we, as believers, dropped out of the culture war and let the secular enemies run rampant. Consequently, the ungodly found the encouragement to boldly speak of their perverse activities. The change came about gradually. Heterosexual politicians didn't announce their bedroom habits in political rallies, nor did heterosexual celebrities "celebrate" their normalcy. But gay ones did, flaunting their reprobate attitude as though it were a badge.

Today, commandeering a flawed rainbow (in most cases missing one of the colors) and celebrating "gay pride," those who practice homosexuality have long left the "closet." And the goal is to now put Christians into the closet, sealing their lips to public speech, prayer, or practice of worship.

People used to be offended—or at least shocked—to see homosexuals holding hands or kissing in public. Now that's accepted, pushed on us in TV series after series. Others pretend to be offended—or at least shocked—when they see Christians praying over a meal in a public restaurant.

In screenwriting courses, I have been told to not overtly express biblical ideas in dialogue, just to hint at the Word by showing the principles through action. This is in faith-based films, where the characters are Christians. Fortunately, some writers and producers expect to see Scripture spoken in scripts, because that what's Christians do—they speak the Word to one another. They exhort others to pray and to seek God for direction. They speak about Jesus. At least we should.

For some, too much silence and compromise has come from not speaking the Word to one another. But why should we keep silent? We have the most blessed message in all the world. Why is it that when we speak it, we are told to keep silent? We are called names, and those who oppose us are considered to have a legitimate complaint against us. But when others speak messages of disbelief, of immorality, and of false ideology, they are celebrated. Yet we are denigrated.

This cultural silencing of Christians in the name of *privatization* or *political correctness* is as insidious as was the attempt to silence the first century Christians. When we study how they handled it, we will know how we should respond to the growing pressure to be quiet about the gospel—the Word of Life. We ought not to let the *cancel culture* movement cancel our message of life.

In *Victory through Light: How to Overcome the Growing Cultural Darkness*, I focused on how naturalistic evolution, relative morality, and political correctness have darkened our culture to the point even Christians are becoming misled by, and eventually engulfed in, cultural darkness. I also covered how to gain victory over that darkness.

Victory through Voice: How to Speak Truth When the Culture Demands Silence explores privatization of the Christian faith and exhorts us to speak the truth in love. Privatization is the cultural push to silence the gospel and force Christians to compromise our values and faith to accommodate sin. We are not allowed to speak freely about the deliverance, grace, love, life, and light that our Lord and Savior Jesus Christ offers to a hurting world.

We are silenced from individual witnessing in public schools and universities, the workplace, the public square, and in the secular entertainment industry. Make no mistake about it: the enforced privatization will get worse, given political trends of the socialistic left. Only intense prayer and the intervention of our holy God can stop what has been going on in this country: the eviction of truth, privatization of faith, and national rebellion against the Triune God.

Privatization is really nothing new. It occurred in the first century church and persisted through church history. It is the devil's attack on believers in order to intimidate, threaten, and dissuade them from sharing the glorious gifts they have received. This book will focus on highlights of that attempt at privatization in the book of Acts and letters of Paul. It will touch briefly on events in church history. It will show today's Christians how to stand up to such pressure, how to speak the truth in love, and how to "soldier on" as did Peter, Stephen, Paul, Silas, and all the early disciples.

The shadows cast by moral relativism and postmodern denial of truth make privatization all the deadlier. If all beliefs are equal (as moral relativism says) and no belief expresses an objective, absolute truth (per postmodernism), then coercing one group to be silent about their beliefs would effectively take them out of the public conversation. Silencing the group that has knowledge of absolute truth and objective moral goodness is detrimental to all. The one message which others need to hear is muzzled. The only voices left are those speaking error.

Example of Detrimental Silence

Imagine a world like this: A group of children play on a jungle gym in the park. Parents and babysitters watch from benches and under shade trees while the children play. Everyone has his or her own idea of what safe play looks like, so no one interferes when one child pushes another down the slide or hops off the seesaw with a child in the air.

One parent notices but is afraid to speak because she's been told before that children need to play, and parents need to let them. So she remains quiet, even when a child falls off the slide and another hits the ground with a bone-shattering thump. When the children cry, she still remains silent because she's been told not to interfere with other people's children.

The child who fell from the top of the slide (being pushed over the edge instead of down the slippery part) lies on the ground unconscious. The child on the seesaw can't stand up. But the parent who noticed, being privatized, doesn't say a word. She takes her child and goes home. By then, the medical help finally arrives, and each case has complications.

This analogy doesn't need any explanation. I'm glad our privatization isn't this extreme, and yet the privatization of faith is much more serious, being of eternal importance.

In my example, it's easy to see that the parent who noticed should have said something—or checked the kids for injuries. That's just what we do. Yet in eternal matters, Christians are told to be silent—that making a stand for true righteousness is "hate speech." For example, if we don't celebrate sin, which our culture does not call sin but rather "an alternate lifestyle," we are accused of being "homophobic."

From the Beginning

As I said earlier, this attempt to silence us has gone on from the beginning of the church. It is the devil's tool when other plans fail. We see it rearing its head in Acts 4:16–18 when the Pharisees employed it to silence the apostles in order to maintain their own hold on the people.

Today, instead of from Pharisees, we see it from the politically correct members of our culture—unbelievers, nominal Christians, career politicians, and secular celebrities. We see it from all those for whom virtue signaling is only an outward show. They speak out on social issues but do nothing to solve problems. At the same time, they presume that alternate views are less moral, less noble, and less tolerant than theirs and, therefore, must be silenced.

In Matthew 23:5–6, Jesus says that the Pharisees do everything to be seen and love the place of prominence. That's the outward show of virtue signaling. Furthermore, in verse 13, he declares,

> "What sorrow awaits you teachers of religious law and you Pharisees. Hypocrites! For you shut the door of the Kingdom of Heaven in people's faces. You won't go in yourselves, and you don't let others enter either." (NLT)

That's the silencing of all who disagree with them and refuse to give them a place of honor.

Acts 4 tells of Peter and John's mock trial in front of the Pharisees. Peter and John had healed a man born lame. The Pharisees were angry, jealous, and afraid that the people would forsake them and follow Peter and John. So they arrested them and held them overnight. Then they challenged them, hoping their threatening tone would cause Peter and John to cower away in timid silence. But Peter, filled with the Holy Spirit, said to them, "Rulers and elders of the people . . . let it be known to all of you and to all the people of Israel, that by the name of Jesus Christ the Nazarene, whom you crucified, whom God raised from the dead—by this name this man stands here before you in good health. (Acts 4:8, 10 NASB)

He even went further to proclaim, "And there is salvation in no one else; for there is no other name under heaven that has been given among mankind by which we must be saved" (v. 12 NASB).

Obviously, that isn't what the Pharisees wanted to hear, especially as they realized that Peter and John were not schooled in Torah as they were, but were simply fishermen. Their only claim to knowledge was that they had been with Jesus. But the Pharisees couldn't deny the man's healing. So they conferred among themselves,

saying, "What are we to do with these men? For the fact that a noteworthy miracle has taken place through them is apparent to all who live in Jerusalem, and we cannot deny it. But so that it will not spread any further among the people, let's warn them not to speak any longer to any person in this name." And when they had summoned them, they commanded them not to speak or teach at all in the name of Jesus. (Acts 4:16–18 NASB)

The devil's ultimate reason for the silence was to stop the message of life, love, and light. But to the Pharisees, it was simply to hold on to their power. And that is the reason for the push for our privatization today. The elite of the culture resist losing their power.

Moreover, the unbelieving world does not want to hear about Jesus, who can set them free from the darkness they live in, who can give them hope from the despair they face, and who can change the miserable life they have chosen for themselves. The secular world does not want others who are in the darkness with them to be enlightened and to find the liberty that is in Christ. The carnal Christian doesn't want to be reminded of eternity or to be confronted with his or her failure to walk in the light they have been given.

Peter and John replied that they had to do what was right in God's eyes, not the Pharisees' eyes. They proclaimed, "[W]e cannot stop speaking about what we have seen and heard" (v. 20 NASB). In other words, they found it impossible to be silent about the truth. And that should be our response today. Not in pride or haughtiness, but in the boldness and love of the Holy Spirit.

The Pharisees threatened them some more, but Peter and John went back to the believers and had a prayer meeting, seeking more boldness to speak the Word, more healings, and signs and wonders in Jesus' name. "[A]nd abundant grace was upon them all" (v. 33 NASB).

That was then and this is now, you may say. But what do we see happening now? Teachers are told to never bring up the name of Jesus, to not bring a Bible to school (or if they do, to hide it from students), to not discuss the Bible in class, and so on.

My Experiences in Education

While I substituted one day as a para in a seventh-grade class-room, the teacher (also a substitute) mentioned the Bible, in the context of the story the class had read. One student piped up, as though he could scare her: "Oooooh, you can't say the word Bible in here." She had a valid answer, and he backed down. But what had he heard in the past that gave him those words and the brashness to speak to a teacher that way?

While teaching non-traditional college students, I was chas-tised by the Dean of a supposedly Christian university's school of professional and graduate studies for agreeing with a student who said that evolution is false and God created the world. It was in the context of critical thinking for argument presentation and identifying one's audience to find common ground.

He accused me of unduly influencing these working adult students with my beliefs in order to coerce them into believing as I do. "You could influence them," he wrote in his scathing review. As though that would be a bad thing. Or as though the atheist teacher doesn't influence students with his or her view. Or as though adult students, several of whom had seen combat, who had jobs and families, could be so easily influenced by one teacher's comments.

Biblical Challenges

When the Old Testament prophet Daniel was challenged to privatize his faith, he refused, choosing instead to continue to pray to God three times a day, as was his custom. He had been set up, but he didn't hide his action behind closed curtains. With windows wide open, he prayed in his chamber, in violation of the law which had been written to ensnare him. As David Jeremiah put it in a televised sermon, "Daniel didn't stand down; he didn't stand aside; and he didn't stand against. He stood up—he stood up for what he believed."

Daniel didn't cower in fear of the demand to be silent. He didn't compromise and try to sneak a prayer in when no one was looking or pretend to pray to the king while praying to God in his heart. He didn't organize a protest against the unfair law. He just did what he always did, in faith and humility. Consequently, God—and the king—honored that stand.

When People Ask about Our Faith

Sometimes, it's easier to witness when people ask us about our faith. If they bring it up, we can relax, thinking we have their permission to speak. It removes that fear of "offending" someone. Peter writes, "Always be ready to give an answer to every man who asks you for a reason for the hope that is in you, with gentleness and fear" (1 Peter 3:15 MEV). If people ask, they want to know.

Obviously, if people do not see our hope as believers, they won't ask us about it. If we fret, worry, cower in fear, complain, bicker, or claim victimhood, people won't realize that we have something special called *faith* and *redemption*. So they won't ask. And we will miss the opportunity to answer.

With respect to giving an answer, 1 Peter 3:16 in the *New Living Translation* reads, "But do this in a gentle and respectful way." We should tell them gently and with respect, with kindness and sincerity—not self-righteously, proudly, or judgmentally. We should tell them with reverence toward God, not emphasis on self. And we should yearn for the opportunity to share our hope with them.

Reflect Further

1. Remember the opening story about my babysitting experience. Think of a time when you did not witness as you now think you should have. Examine your reasons for not witnessing. What can you do about it now?

2. In John 13:37–38, Jesus predicted Peter's denial of him. That denial is recorded in Matthew 26:69–75. Examine Peter's reason for denying Jesus. Was it valid at the time?

3. In Mark 16:5–7, an angel instructs the ladies at the empty tomb to give a message to the disciples and to Peter. John 21:15–19 records a special dialogue between the risen Jesus and Peter. Based on these Scriptures, we can see that Peter was given a second chance. Can we expect the same?

4. In Acts 1:15–22, Peter takes charge and leads in choosing a replacement for Judas Iscariot, who betrayed Jesus and hung himself. Note that Peter stood and spoke on the day of Pentecost when the 120 were filled with the Holy Spirit, as seen in Acts 2. Can we expect a ministry if God calls us? Even if we fail?

5. We know that not everyone is called to preach or lead in an assembly. But should we witness to friends and strangers, as God leads? See 1 Peter 3:15; and Colossians 4:6.

6. In what other ways can we show the gospel to others, even if the culture tells us to be silent? (For example, Samaritan's Purse set up a tent hospital complex in New York City in 2020 to help treat victims of the Coronavirus. I read several articles that exposed the attacks on them and the demands that they leave, simply because they are a Christian group which is known to not celebrate the LGBTQ lifestyle. Their continued medical assistance is an example of showing the gospel.) List things you can do to witness by your actions.

7. Daniel 6 narrates Daniel's experience before and in the lions' den. Do you think it was easier for people in Bible times than for us now to stand up for faith and speak the truth? Why or why not?

8. Jeremiah experienced persecution for speaking truth in his prophecies. At one point, he decided to stop speaking. But he found that his silence was unbearable and that the Word became "as a burning fire shut up in my bones" (Jeremiah 20:9 KJV). Have you ever felt that if you didn't speak to someone about the Lord, you would melt from the inside out, as Jeremiah implied? Describe what happened.

9. In Acts 1:8, we are promised the Holy Spirit's boldness to speak the Word and to witness wherever we are. Does this apply to all believers or only a select few?

10. What's the worst thing that has ever happened to you as a result of sharing your faith with someone? What is the best thing?

CHAPTER 2

Commanded to Keep Silent

IN ACTS 4, WE READ THAT the Pharisees warned and threatened the disciples, commanding them not to speak about Jesus in public. While some people may tell us not to witness in public, there is another force that sometimes causes us to keep quiet.

Our own inhibitions can stop us from sharing Christ. I remember a time when my first son was born, healthy and screaming. The lady in the hospital room next to mine had had a still birth. When I heard that, my heart ached for her. I cried. Immediately the Lord quickened to my mind the verse, "Weep with them that weep" (Romans 12:15 KJV). He urged me to go and just sit with her and weep.

This was another time I failed to minister God's love. I argued myself out of it, thinking that she might misunderstand, or she might feel offended, or I might be invading her privacy. After all, I didn't know her, so I wasn't supposed to know what had happened to her. (This was years before the multi-page, oft-repeated "right to privacy" notice.)

I told myself that if she asked me in, I would go, but . . . I was too timid even to take that first step and ask her. I should have followed the Lord's direction, knowing that if he directed me to do it, he would take care of all my concerns about it. But instead I sat in my hospital bed and prayed for her while I waited on the nurse to bring my baby into the room.

I lost a chance to bless someone else that day. Possibly lost a chance to speak to her about the comfort and salvation that is in Christ. And I lost a blessing for myself—a blessing that comes when one obeys the Word and the leading of the Holy Spirit.

Scriptural Reactions

When I look at the book of Acts, I see quite the opposite reaction to the needs of people. Yes, the lame man in Acts 3 was begging for money when Peter and John healed him. He did not specifically ask for a healing, but Peter told him directly what he could do for him: "I do not have silver and gold, but what I do have I give to you: In the name of Jesus Christ the Nazarene, walk!" (Acts 3:6 NASB).

Peter didn't stop with words. He lifted the man up by his right hand, and as the man responded to that lifting, his feet and ankle bones received strength. And this man who had never walked, never used the muscles in his legs, stood, walked, and leaped, praising God (Acts 3:7–8).

For that healing and the preaching afterward (partly in response to the Pharisees' questions), Peter and John were commanded not to speak in Jesus' name. They chose to obey God, though, and "great grace was upon them all" (Acts 4:33 KJV).

The result was that more people came for healing. Multitudes were added to the believers, both men and women, and from the region around Jerusalem came a multitude, bringing their sick and those with demons. And "they were healed every one" (Acts 5:16 KJV).

For some reason, Christians in the United States have come to not expect healings like this. Perhaps we believe that God no longer heals that way. Or perhaps we just lack the faith to lay hold of his mighty power. God forbid that it's because we fear possible repercussions from those in political authority.

It didn't take long for the high priest and the sect of Sadducees with him to respond in "indignation" (Acts 5:17 KJV). They threw Peter and John into the "common prison" (v. 18 KJV). Isn't that reason enough to keep quiet—to stay out of jail? Not for the first century Christians. I pray that we in this twenty-first century would have the same boldness.

What Do We Face?

So far, in the United States, we don't have to fear imprisonment for our faith, though the Covid-19 event brought threats of jail time. Some pastors were jailed for holding church services when the governors or mayors commanded them not to. (The closing of churches was not a "law" legislated by Congress or an executive order by the President. It was at the whim of lesser political leaders who issued dictatorial orders purported to be for "the people's good.")

Moreover, a state agency harassed and discriminated against a Christian realtor for putting John 3:16 on her website and including a message, "Jesus loves you," in her email signature. She was forced to quit her job, and her employer was coerced into blacklisting her and reporting on her "religious" conduct to the state agency.

The anti-Christian organization Freedom from Religion Foundation has hassled and badgered leaders who have called for a day of prayer regarding Covid-19 and who have offered prayers for victims of the virus. It seems that merely saying,

"I'll pray for you," is enough to send that organization into war mode and to trigger lawsuits.

The mayor of Greenville, Mississippi, ordered that churches were non-essential and could not even have drive-in services. Consequently, when less than twenty people gathered in cars in the parking lot to listen to the service on the radio, windows up, the police department issued $500 tickets.

Another church was also harassed. After then President Trump's Department of Justice spoke against the order and fines, the Mississippi governor stepped in. This case ended well because the mayor conceded, waived the fines, and said that churches could meet like that as long as car windows remained up.

The interesting thing to note is that when churches were ordered to close, department stores remained open. When drive-in services were banned, drive-in restaurants were allowed to remain open. And who has ever ordered food via drive-through or gone to a drive-in restaurant and NOT rolled down the window—at least to pay and get the food?

Thus, these rulings were clearly designed to persecute Christians. True, we should take appropriate actions with respect to our age, overall health, family needs, and the safety and welfare of others. But fear of getting sick should not replace our faith in God to sustain us and to work his will in our lives.

In the United States, outside of the recent virus outbreak, what punishments do Christians face in this third decade of the 21st century? Lawsuits for refusal to celebrate sin. Having one's business ruined and bankrupted because of a stand for God's righteous order. Receiving negative publicity by the liberal media, libelous and slanderous claims, vandalism, verbal abuse, and false accusations. Pressure—economic and otherwise—to conform to politically correct acceptance and celebration of perversion, rebellion, and sin. And on top of that, calls by the far left to send us to re-education camps or jail. One PBS lawyer was fired for saying on a video that the left should send the children of republicans to re-education camps. Others called for such treatment (and worse) in Twitter posts.

However, fear of these things should not paralyze us and silence our voice.

Biblical Re-education

What occurred in Acts 5 when Peter and John were jailed? "But the angel of the Lord by night opened the prison doors, and brought them forth, and said, Go, stand and speak in the temple to the people all the words of this life" (vv. 19–20 KJV). An angel let them out of jail!

Can we expect divine and miraculous intercession if we face unjust punishment for witnessing about the Lord? I believe we can. I think that sometimes we don't see it because we aren't looking for it or expecting it. And sometimes, the miracle is what happened to the apostle Paul later on— survival and ministry in the prison. Even if we suffer the full consequences of speaking about Jesus, it is a testimony that he is worth whatever sacrifice our society imposes on us.

Peter writes of this in his first epistle:

> For this is commendable, if because of conscience toward God a person endures grief, suffering unjustly. For what credit is it if when you are being beaten for your sins you patiently endure? But if when doing good and suffering for it, you patiently endure, this is favorable before God. For to this you were called, because Christ suffered for us, leaving us an example, that you should follow His steps. (1 Peter 2:19–21 MEV)

Peter and John obeyed the angel that set them free and went back into the temple and taught. I have to laugh that the high priest and Sadducees didn't realize that Peter and John were in the temple. They were so set on stopping them that they shirked their own duties in the temple. It's funny that they sent to the prison for them, found out they were not there but in the temple teaching, and they were worried. See Acts 5:21–27.

So the Jewish leaders brought the apostles before the Sanhedrin so the high priest could question them. Here's the accusation: "Did we not strictly command you not to teach in this name? Yet now you have filled Jerusalem with your teaching, and you intend to bring on us this Man's blood" (v. 28 MEV). The high priest was alarmed that the apostles were not only spreading the gospel of Jesus throughout Jerusalem, but that they also were holding the Jewish leaders accountable for their part in Jesus' death.

Earlier, those same leaders had proclaimed, "His blood be on us, and on our children" (Matthew 27:25 KJV). They knew they were guilty. They knew that the thirty pieces of silver they had paid Judas Iscariot was "the price of blood" (Matthew 27:6 KJV). They could not deny their guilt, but they didn't want to be reminded of it by these apostles who spoke the truth.

The apostles answered them plainly. To the first charge, they said, "We must obey God rather than men" (Acts 5:29 NASB). To the second charge, they answered in truth:

> The God of our fathers raised Jesus, whom you killed by hanging on a tree. God exalted this Man to His right hand to be a Ruler and a Savior, to give repentance to Israel and forgiveness of sins. We are His witnesses to these words, as is the Holy Spirit whom God has given to those who obey Him. (vv. 30–32 MEV)

In effect, what they said was this: "His blood *is* on you. You killed him. But the God you claim to worship raised him from the dead and made him King and Savior, so that you could be forgiven of your sins." Wow. Powerful preaching. Were these Jewish leaders convicted to salvation? No. Rather, they "were cut to the heart and took counsel to kill them" (v. 33 MEV).

In verses 34–39, we see the wise counsel of a Pharisee named Gamaliel. It is interesting to note that the apostle Paul (who starts out as Saul, the enemy of the church) later said that Gamaliel had been his teacher (Acts 22:3). Gamaliel makes a good point, to which the Jews give heed. He cautions that if "this work is of men, it will come to nothing; but if it is of God, you cannot overthrow it—lest you even be found to fight against God" (Acts 5:38–39 NKJV).

The fact that they listened to Gamaliel's advice proves that they suspected the work was of God. Otherwise, why back down? If they knew of a certainty that Jesus was not who he claimed to be—if they knew of a certainty that he had not been raised from the dead—they would have had to stand their ground. If they were fully convinced the work of the apostles was not of God, they would have had to eradicate it, even if that meant killing those who spoke it. They would have been assured that the message of the gospel was error and idolatry.

But they lacked that certainty, because in their hearts they were convicted. They could not dispute that Jesus was the Son of God, alive again, having fulfilled the Scriptures. But they rejected the salvation he offered. They refused to repent and acknowledge the truth. They chose the darkness over the light, as Jesus had said: "And the judgment is based on this fact: God's light came into the world, but people loved the darkness more than the light, for their actions were evil. All who do evil hate the light and refuse to go near it for fear their sins will be exposed" (John 3:19–20 NLT).

That principle, in evidence in the first century, is still evident today. From the beginning of Jesus' life on earth it was so, for he was

> the true Light that, coming into the world, enlightens every person. He was in the world, and the world came into being through Him, and yet the world did not know Him. He came to His own, and His own people did not accept Him. (John 1:9–11 NASB)

That consequence is still obvious today. Those who reject Jesus—the true Light—stumble around in the darkness of their sins and rebellion. Our culture grows darker and darker, and it demands more strongly that we be silent. Those of the secular culture do not want to hear the message of light, life, and love. Does that mean we should stop speaking it? No. We must continue speaking the truth in love, even if it costs us more and more, just as it did the early apostles.

The wisdom of Gamaliel is not found in the unbelievers today. This is because Gamaliel believed (mentally, at least) that God exists and works in the lives of his people Israel. But most political leaders today, especially on the left, along with many religious leaders in pulpits, reject the reality of God and his sovereign work. Our dark culture today does not consider it wise to let Christians alone and see if the work will fade away or be established by God.

For the apostles, the wisdom of Gamaliel was accepted briefly, but not without some violence. In Acts 5:40, we see that the Jewish leaders reinforced their command with a beating, and commanded that they should not speak in Jesus' name. Then they let them go.

What did the apostles do? They surely didn't comply. They didn't tape their mouths shut. They didn't cry and moan and act like victims. Verse 41 tells us clearly that they "departed from the presence of the council, rejoicing that they were counted worthy to suffer shame for his name" (KJV). And they kept preaching and teaching about Jesus Christ, "daily in the temple, and in every house" (v. 42 KJV).

They "ceased not." They refused to be silenced. We can and should make that same choice. Not in the spirit of anger or autonomy but in obedience to our Lord Jesus Christ and with love for others—just as the early apostles did.

The beatings we receive may be verbal or economic rather than physical. Our culture professes to abhor violence, so it doesn't use whips and rods to physically beat up those whom it rejects for being "politically incorrect." But whatever comes in suffering for Christ, can we endure it? Can we rejoice in it?

Will we be called fools? Will we be mocked and considered uneducated, in spite of possible college degrees? Yes. The world will lightly esteem us. But does that matter? The late Justice Scalia said,

> God assumed from the beginning that the wise of the world would view Christians as fools . . . and He has not been disappointed. Devout Christians are destined to be regarded as fools in modern society. We are fools for Christ's sake. We must pray for courage to endure the scorn of the sophisticated world. If I have brought any message today, it is this: Have the courage to have your wisdom regarded as stupidity. Be fools for Christ. And have the courage to suffer the contempt of the sophisticated world.[1]

Of course, to be regarded as fools, we must be recognized as devout Christians. This applies to the average, born-again believer as well as to ministers and those in position of authority in the church. In the early church, the apostles were attacked. A short time later, even the believers were sought out for arrest. See Acts 8:1–3.

Reflect Further

1. What if you're not a teacher, preacher, evangelist, or speaker? Does the instruction to share the gospel even apply to you? Read Mark 16:17–18. When Jesus said, "These miraculous signs will accompany those who believe" (Mark 16:17 NLT), he was speaking of all believers, not just the remaining eleven disciples. Notice that casting out demons, speaking in new languages and with a new creation tongue, certain miracles of surviving venomous beasts and poisonings, and healings were given as signs of those who believe. Consider how these things might apply to present-day ordinary believers. Do you believe that you can have these signs following you?

2. We can glean many lessons from the origin of the church, recorded in Acts 2. One hundred twenty people gathered—men and women, the disciples, and other believers. On the day of Pentecost, Peter preached to a large crowd living in and gathered to Jerusalem, and approximately three thousand were saved (Acts 2:41). Notice his words in Acts 2:39. Does "all that are afar off" (KJV) refer to time as well as distance? What about "as many as the Lord our God shall call" (v. 39 KJV)? The promise of verse 38 is to you, whosoever you are that have been called. And if that promise is to you, so is the promise of Mark

16:17–18. Does that thrill you and fill you with courage to share the gospel?

3. Read Romans 12:4–12. There we see that we have different ministries, gifts, and offices. However, we all have the instruction to live our lives with love, joy, peace, patience, and honesty. We are to give, bless, and comfort. What are some ways you can minister to others with your life, by your actions and attitudes? Are you striving to be an epistle of good news? See 2 Corinthians 3:2–3.

4. Ephesians 4:15 tells us that we grow up into Christ as we speak the truth in love. Philippians 2:14–16 shows that our lives can testify of salvation. Whether by speech or action, our motivation should be love for others and obedience to the Word of God. What do you think Jude 1:22–23 means in terms of our culture today? Are *showing compassion* and *snatching from judgment* two different approaches? How would these be used today? Have you known people who are emotionally fragile and need to be reproved gently? And others whose stubbornness requires stern chastening to get through to them?

5. Read Matthew 10:28–31. There, Jesus explains our worth and instructs us regarding godly fear. Consider these questions: Who is able to kill the body? Who is able to kill the soul? Do you understand what he is saying in these verses?

6. There are other Scriptures stating that God knows how many hairs are on our head, as a measure of our importance

to Christ. Do you believe you are that important to him? Does he indeed know how many hairs you have? Or is that a figure of speech to express your value?

7. Romans 10:9–10 makes it clear that if we confess our faith in Christ, we are saved (born-again). In Matthew 10:32–33, we see a warning about denying Christ. What happens if we fear people so much that we later deny believing in Jesus? Do we lose our salvation? Or do we simply lose rewards and the best that God has for us? See 2 Timothy 2:11–13.

8. Old Testament writers looked to God for the right words to speak. See Psalm 51:15 and Jeremiah 1:9. Whether we are under persecution or simply witnessing to friends, does it take the anointing of the Lord for us to boldly speak the truth of the gospel?

CHAPTER 3

Silenced by Death

NOW THAT WE'VE established that it's the responsibility of every believer to share Christ in the way that God gives him or her to do, let's look at the life of Stephen. Chosen as one of the men to serve tables and hand out food to needy widows, Stephen found himself called by God to preach (Acts 6:1–6). As a result,

> Stephen, full of faith and power, did great wonders and miracles among the people. Then some men rose up . . . disputing with Stephen. But they were not able to withstand the wisdom and the Spirit by which he spoke. (vv. 8–10 MEV)

In Our Day

Imagine a man serving in a food line at a shelter or soup kitchen in the inner city. Such a man is responsible perhaps for cooking the food, serving it equally to those who come to eat, and cleaning up after the meal. No one expects him to preach or even know much about the Bible. His role is one of service.

Pretend the man then goes to church and, in Jesus' name, does miracles of healing and deliverance. So the clergy in charge at the church start quizzing him about how or why he could do that. They accuse him of encroaching on their territory. They dispute with him. But he answers them from the Word of God in a way that they cannot refute. He knows his Bible.

How do they react to this "outsider" who seems more knowledgeable than they? What will they do to protect their territory?

In Stephen's Day

In Stephen's day, they hired people to accuse him of blasphemy against Moses and God. They stirred up the officials, caught him, and brought him to a hearing before the high priest and others. They hired false witnesses who claimed he blasphemed the temple and the law (Acts 6:11–14).

Did Stephen back down? Did he apologize? Did he respond in anger and demand his rights? No. No. And no. In fact, his face lit up with the glory of God: "And all who were sitting in the Council stared at him, and they saw his face, which was like the face of an angel" (Acts 6:15 NASB).

The high priest, officiating the mock trial, asked if those things (the false accusations) were true (Acts 7:1). Stephen launched into an awesome sermon retracing Israel's history and highlighting God's work among the people. Read Acts 7:2–53. Imagine our hypothetical soup-kitchen worker rehearsing church history and concluding with an accusation against unbelieving clergy who taught only a distorted social gospel.

The religious leaders of Israel responded with hatred. "Now when they heard this, they were infuriated, and they began gnashing their teeth at him" (v. 54 NASB). Now, they didn't literally bite him, as a pack of wild dogs would do. But they were grinding their teeth—clenching their jaws in anger and wrath. Today, we might describe it like this: their jaws rippled and "they shook their fists at him in rage" (v. 54 NLT).

Did he then back down? No. "But he, being full of the Holy Spirit, gazed into heaven and saw the glory of God, and Jesus standing at the right hand of God, and said, 'Look! I see the heavens opened and the Son of Man standing at the right hand of God!'" (vv. 55–56 NKJV).

You would think that would cause them to stop and consider that maybe he was right. Maybe what he said about Jesus was really true. But, no.

> Then they cried out with a loud voice, stopped their ears, and ran at him with one accord; and they cast him out of the city, and stoned him. And the witnesses laid down their clothes at the feet of a young man named Saul. (vv. 57–58 NKJV)

Can you hear them screaming "Shut up!" as they covered their ears to show that they would not listen to him any longer? Can you see them swarming him, an angry mob, driving him to the alley and picking up stones, bricks, and whatever objects they could find? Can you see them removing their heavy coats and tossing them at Saul's feet so they could throw better? Can you see them hurling those rocks and heavy objects at Stephen, hitting him in his head, chest, and legs?

Did Stephen cry out for them to stop or to show mercy? No. As they stoned him, he called upon God and spoke words similar to what Jesus spoke from the cross: "Lord Jesus, receive my spirit" (v. 59 NKJV). Compare with Luke 23:46.

Stephen then kneeled down. He didn't fall down. He intentionally knelt. And he cried with a loud voice—not a timid, weak one: "Lord, do not charge them with this sin" (v. 60 NKJV). In his dying words, he spoke forgiveness, as did Jesus. Compare with Luke 23:34.

Can you imagine how that would have cut them to the heart? Visualize Saul standing there, observing in an official capacity. Acts 8:1 tells us that he had consented to the death of Stephen. Of course, he didn't think of it as murder. He and the other Pharisees thought they were defending their God. But their religion had no life in it. They had turned away from the light and had sacrificed the truth.

Would Stephen have been better off to have apologized for "offending them"? Then he could have gone on serving tables and working miracles (behind their backs, of course). True faith doesn't "cool it," hide in a closet, or apologize. It does not back down. It does not surrender. It does not compromise.

Our Message

We have a message that can set people free and give eternal life. We have a message that exalts the God of creation and brings glory to the Lord of Redemption. As Saul (later renamed Paul) proclaims in Romans 1:16, "For I am not ashamed of the gospel of Christ. For it is the power of God for salvation to everyone who believes" (MEV).

The world—our darkening culture—needs this Word. Every believer has been given a "ministry of reconciliation" (2 Corinthians 5:18 KJV). According to 2 Corinthians 5:17–18,

> This means that anyone who belongs to Christ has become a new person. The old life is gone; a new life has begun! And all of this is a gift from God, who brought us back to himself through Christ. And God has given us this task of reconciling people to him. (NLT)

We aren't all evangelists, but we have a responsibility to the ones God places in our lives and in our paths. We have a responsibility to exhort them to be reconciled to God by faith in Jesus Christ. And we testify to them of our own reconciliation, sharing with them the good news of forgiveness of sins, new life in Christ, and the reality of eternal life.

Persecution by Religious Leaders

Stephen's death was the first by "religious" leaders (self-righteous but unsaved). More followed, along with imprisonments, as we see Saul persecuting the church (which Acts 9:5 NASB describes as persecuting Jesus):

> Saul was one of the witnesses, and he agreed completely with the killing of Stephen. A great wave of persecution began that day, sweeping over the church in Jerusalem; and all the believers except the apostles were scattered through the regions of Judea and Samaria. (Some devout men came and buried Stephen with great mourning.) But Saul was going everywhere to destroy the church. He went from house to house, dragging out both men and women to throw them into prison. (Acts 8:1-3 NLT)

In that scattering, the Christians carried the Word and preached salvation everywhere they went (v. 4). Jesus had told them that they would be witnesses "both in Jerusalem, and in all Judæa, and in Samaria, and unto the uttermost part of the earth" (Acts 1:8 KJV).

Saul Becomes Paul

Saul continued on this "warpath" of sorts, fully believing that he was doing God's work. (See Acts 9:1–2; 26:9–11; and Philippians 3:5–6.) While he was on that journey, God stopped him in his tracks, in a most spectacular way:

> As he went he drew near Damascus, and suddenly a light from heaven shone around him. He fell to the ground and heard a voice saying to him, "Saul, Saul, why do you persecute Me?" He said, "Who are You, Lord?" The Lord said, "I am Jesus, whom you are persecuting. It is hard for you to kick against the goads." Trembling and astonished, he said, "Lord, what will You have me do?" The Lord said to him, "Rise up and go into the city, and you will be told what you must do." (Acts 9:3–6 MEV)

His conversion was sudden, dramatic, and miraculous. And it was effective, as Paul later writes in Galatians 1:11–17 and 1 Timothy 1:11–16. To "kick against the goads" means to resist the testimony of those speaking truth about Christ—to repel the conviction of the Holy Spirit.

Note that Jesus appeared to him as a bright light. This is significant as we compare it to John 1:4–12 and 3:19–21. Jesus came as the true Light. He came first to his own—Israel, of which nation Saul/Paul was a religious leader. For the most part, the leaders of Israel rejected Jesus. However, "To all who believed him and accepted him, he gave the right to become children of God" (John 1:12 NLT).

Furthermore, Jesus said that those who do evil hate the light, but "those who do what is right come to the light so others can see that they are doing what God wants" (John 3:21 NLT). Thus, the true Light appeared to Saul. He received that Light, came to that Light, and became a child of God. He was later renamed Paul. And he did what God wanted.

The Importance of Light

This is how important the light is. The light is essential to our salvation and our Christian life. We cannot stay in the darkness and expect to please God. We come to the light and then face the persecution that the darkness will bring. But we face it, knowing that light triumphs.

So Paul's life changed and he immediately stopped persecuting the church. You can read Acts 9:7–30 to see the results of his encounter with Jesus, the Light. He went to his hometown, Tarsus, and was taught by the Holy Spirit for three years before he went back to Jerusalem and began his ministry and missionary journeys.

In Paul's retelling of his experience on the road to Damascus, he says to King Agrippa,

> "At midday, O king, along the road I saw a light from heaven, brighter than the sun, shining around me and those who journeyed with me. And when we all had fallen to the ground, I heard a voice speaking to me." (Acts 26:13–14 NKJV)

In this account, we read more of what Jesus said to him, which might have been on that road or after Paul received the Holy Spirit at the ministering of Ananias. (It's interesting that when Paul retells his conversion, he doesn't let himself get bogged down in details, but trims where he must to make it flow well for the listener. See also Acts 22:4–11. This serves as a mark of credibility. Who of us retells a personal experience exactly the same way to different audiences? Telling it word-for-word is a clear indication that it is a memorized sales pitch or a lie.)

In Acts 26, Paul tells King Agrippa that Jesus commissioned him to the Gentiles,

> "to open their eyes, so they may turn from darkness to light and from the power of Satan to God. Then they will receive forgiveness for their sins and be given a place among God's people, who are set apart by faith in me [Christ]." (v. 18 NLT)

The phrase "given a place" is translated as "receive an inheritance" in other versions. But the key point is that the presence of divine light dispels darkness.

Paul's Function in the Church

Since Paul started out as Saul, a Pharisee, why didn't he function as a bridge, bringing the Jewish leaders into the truth? You would think that they would see his example and follow. But not so. They rejected Christ for the same reason that the world rejects him. To accept him means we have to admit we are sinners in need of the Savior. To accept him means to turn from the darkness of our ways to the light of his way. And those religious leaders did not want to do that.

Instead, they hounded and persecuted Paul, chasing him away from mission fields and getting him thrown into Roman prisons. That's basically the story of Acts 13—28.

Persecution by Secular Leaders

In the early church, the Jewish leaders were not the only enemy. The unbelieving Roman leaders also badgered the believers. King Herod vexed certain ones of the church and "killed James the brother of John with the sword" (Acts 12:2 KJV).

When he saw that made the Jews happy, he decided to also take Peter. He arrested him and "put him in prison and handed him over to four squads of soldiers to guard him, intending to bring him before the people after the Passover" (v. 4 MEV). He most likely planned to kill him at that time. The whole culture was rebelling against the Savior, Jesus Christ, and against all those who spoke his truth.

But God had different plans. He broke Peter out of jail (see Acts 12:6–19). When Herod found out that Peter had escaped, he commanded that the four squads (sixteen soldiers) be put to death. Not long afterward, Herod exalted himself, and the people claimed his voice was that of a god and not a man. For a moment, Herod must have felt grand.

However, that quickly ended when an "angel of the Lord struck him, because he did not give God the glory. And he was eaten by worms and died" (Acts 12:23 MEV). Note that he didn't get eaten by worms in the grave after death and burial. He was eaten by worms while alive, and that killed him. A gruesome death indeed.

The unbelieving world is looking for a man to praise and exalt over them. They are primed to accept the Antichrist, who will reveal himself in the great tribulation. He also will meet a disastrous end (Revelation 19:20).

In Herod's day, "the word of God spread and increased" (Acts 12:24 MEV). Even a powerful secular king could not stop the testimony of believers. Should we let politicians stop our testimonies today?

We have a slight advantage over the first century believers. We have the full revelation, which was not yet written when they lived. Paul's letters came some thirty years after the church began, and John wrote the book of Revelation around A.D. 96—sixty years after the church began. Moreover, we also have what the early church had: the Holy Spirit—the Spirit of Truth—whom Jesus promised and sent, and who is available to all who believe (Acts 2:39).

Persecution in Our Day

However, we dare not think that we are above persecution. Our culture grows darker and darker as sins multiply in our land. Nominal Christians oppose us because we stand for the righteousness of God, unafraid to call sin "sin" and unwilling to compromise with politically correct sins such as abortion and homosexuality. We stand for the reality of the gospel they have forsaken. They've accepted another gospel, which is not really a gospel (good news) but is deception and falsehood.

The unbelieving culture hates us because we point out the one and only way to God, and they want to either make their own way or simply reject God. As mentioned before, they hate the light and prefer the darkness where they think they can hide their sins. But the light which shines in the darkness cannot be overcome by the darkness. The light will expose sin.

But sin can dim the light of our testimony. It can muffle our voices.

Reflect Further

1. Jesus warned the disciples about what awaited them. Read Matthew 10:16–20; John 15:18–21; and 16:2. List the things Jesus said they would suffer. What promise does he give to encourage them to speak the truth even in captivity?

2. In John 15:21, Jesus says, "They will do all this to you because of me, for they have rejected the one who sent me" (NLT). Read 1 John 2:15–17. Do unbelievers "love the world"? Why are believers not "of the world"? When John instructs us to not love the world, is he speaking of the people or the world's culture? Explain.

3. Christ rejecters say that the disciples hid Jesus' body and pretended that he rose. However, he was seen after his resurrection, and that is well documented. Does it then seem logical that they would insist on his resurrection if he had not been raised—and through that, face persecution? Who would willingly be persecuted for a lie? Read 1 Corinthians 4:11–13. Would Paul willingly suffer those things if he was not convinced that Jesus rose from the dead?

4. Jesus' resurrection is a fact (1 Corinthians 15:20). Gene Edward Veith writes, "Christianity, like science, has to do

with physical reality, with the realm of facts."[1] With that in mind, when Christians are being persecuted for faith in Christ, are they not really being persecuted for believing in physical reality? Do you think the world would admit to this?

5. Read John 17:14–20. Do these verses make it clear that the warning about suffering applies to all believers in all centuries, even to today? Can you think of a reason why this would not apply?

6. Read Romans 8:16–17. What do we have to gain by suffering with Christ—that is, taking a stand in the face of a world/culture that hates our message of light, love, and eternal life?

7. In 2 Timothy 3:12, Paul guarantees we will face persecution. But we live in a different culture today than that of the first century. List some of the ways we suffer today when the culture rejects us and our message.

8. Do you think our culture simply doesn't agree with us, or is it that they hate us? See John 3:16–21. Do they hate us as individuals or hate the light that is in us—or both?

9. Read 1 John 4:4–6. Do we already have a victory over the worldly culture? Explain.

CHAPTER 4

Silenced by Sin

WE CAN LOOK AT the life of King David to see how sin can mar our testimony and cause us to keep silent out of shame. This holds true even when we confuse our sin for love, or see it as an acceptable behavior. This wrongly defined and misguided love can wreak havoc on the individual, the family, and the society. Read 2 Samuel, chapter 11. There we see the well-known story of David and Bathsheba.

We all recognize that what gripped David at first was lust, not godly love. He saw a woman that his flesh desired. He found out that she was the wife of one of his best and most faithful soldiers, one of those listed as "David's mightiest warriors" (1 Chronicles 11:11, 41 NLT). But he sent for her anyway.

And she, knowing the power of the king, came. Was she blameless? I always wondered why she was "washing herself" in public view. Surely she knew that people—even the king—could see her on that rooftop. And not just any king, but a man after God's own heart (1 Samuel 13:14).

So, they had their night of pleasure. But it was sin—not love. And God made sure their sin found them out (Numbers 32:23). Bathsheba conceived.

Short-term Consequences

In that day, they didn't have early detection pregnancy kits. It usually took at least four weeks (or more) to really confirm pregnancy. Even then, one couldn't be sure that it wasn't just stress disrupting the normal cycle. Consequently, after a month or so, she sends word to David.

He's in a pickle now. He can't admit what happened, so he decides to be deceptive and set it up as though her husband is the father. Without DNA testing, that's a workable solution. Just get Uriah home for a few nights and—problem solved.

However, Uriah, faithful warrior that he is, refuses to go home to his wife, even for a night. (I guess they didn't take R & R back then.) I wonder why David didn't simply order him to go home. Perhaps that wasn't part of the command structure.

At this point, David experiences a supreme conflict. If Bathsheba delivers a baby as Uriah's wife, she is subject to stoning since everyone knows Uriah was absent all that time and couldn't be the baby's father. David's plan to rescue her testimony has failed because Uriah wouldn't go home. Thus, her adultery will be known. And David is implicated. Under the law, they could both be stoned.

The pro-abortion person would say, "We have the perfect solution." They might even argue that in this case, it wouldn't have mattered since the baby died anyway. Thus, what difference would it have made?

But abortion only removes the consequences of sin. It does not remove the guilt, the penalty for, or the long-term shame of it. It heaps further sin upon the sin, compounding the guilt. Only the grace and forgiveness of God removes the guilt, penalty, and shame.

Nonetheless, David compounded his guilt with a different kind of murder. He arranged to have Uriah deliberately killed in battle. However, that did not remove his sin of adultery, though on the surface it worked: he could appropriately marry Bathsheba and pretend the child was from their lawful union. (Didn't he know that the people of the kingdom would be counting months and figure it out?) Bathsheba mourned for her husband the traditional thirty days, so when she married David, she was probably almost three months along. Six months later, she bore a son.

David's solution did not meet with God's approval. In 2 Samuel 11:27, we read, "But the thing that David had done displeased the Lord" (KJV). The Hebrew word translated "displeased" means "was evil in the eyes of" the Lord.

How could David, a man after God's own heart, do evil? By letting his flesh deceive him into thinking lust was love. Or perhaps he simply sought, at first, to satisfy his flesh, thinking that everything would go back to normal afterwards.

He could have gone to any of his wives or concubines, but he desired this woman, Bathsheba, the wife of one of his men of valor. As King of Israel, he thought he had a right to her. So, he would have her. Was he sorry later? Yes. Did he repent? Yes. Did all the consequences go away? No.

Our culture would tell us that David's attraction to Bathsheba was love and, therefore, okay. I have no doubt that David grew to love Bathsheba, since it was her son Solomon whom he chose to succeed him, rather than sons from earlier marriages.

In fact, her son Solomon and her son Nathan are both in the lineage of Christ. (See Matthew 1:6 and Luke 3:31.) This shows how God's grace can cover sin. And we know from Psalm 51 that David did indeed repent, just as we see in 2 Samuel 12:13: "Then David confessed to Nathan, 'I have sinned against the Lord.' Nathan replied, 'Yes, but the Lord has forgiven you, and you won't die for this sin'" (NLT). (This was the prophet Nathan. I believe that David named one of Bathsheba's sons "Nathan" in honor of this great prophet.) Read 2 Samuel 12:1–25 for the immediate results of David's sin.

Long-term Consequences

Though David found forgiveness with the Lord, the consequences of and judgment for his sin followed. Notice in 2 Samuel 12:14, what God considers part of the sin—a tarnished testimony: "However, because by this deed you have given great occasion to the enemies of the Lord to blaspheme, the child also who is born to you shall surely die" (NKJV).

When we sin, we give the enemy ammunition to use against us and against the gospel. David would have to bear the shame of his sin the rest of his life. His testimony was tarnished, and he knew it. I believe that his remembrance of his own sin paralyzed him from taking action against his other sons when they needed correction. How could he discipline or judge his sons for committing sexual sin when he himself had done so?

Consequences Today

And don't we find ourselves in that predicament today? I am fully convinced that one of the reasons many church leaders do not preach against fornication and other sexual sins is because they have compromised in that area themselves.

Sixty years ago, the majority of young women were virgins when they married. Now, only a minority of teens are still virgins, even before marriage. Many Christian couples co-habit before the wedding—just to be sure they are really compatible, as if that were an acceptable reason. How common is it for a baby or two to precede the nuptial vows? This acceptance of sexual sins carries with it grave consequences for our society.

This lack of clear teaching about sexual purity has given rise to the abortion industry in this nation and in the world. The Worldometers.info site, using World Health Organization (WHO) statistics, show that abortion was the leading cause of death globally in 2020. Abortion killed more than 42.5 million babies, making it higher than other causes of death.[1]

With 40 to 50 million abortions per year, the cumulative total is staggering. The daily total is around 125,000 globally. These numbers alone should cause us to weep in deep remorse and repentance.

For perspective, go to the *Worldometers* website, https://www.worldometers.info/, and scroll down to the section labeled "Health." The live counter shows real time estimates based on reliable statistics provided by WHO and other sources. You can click on the blue words "this year" and change the counting to "today." The "Abortions" add up quickly, with more than one per second, faster than any other cause of death listed—including communicable diseases, malaria, cancer, alcohol, and traffic accidents.

In fact, the only things in that section clicking faster than abortions are *Cigarettes smoked*, and *Money spent on illegal drugs*.

Watch the number of abortions speed by. Each increase in the number is a baby killed in the womb, a child not allowed to live and reach his or her potential. There is also a mother who someday will most likely face remorse and guilt, a mother who will need to hear about the grace and forgiveness of God available through Christ Jesus. But our nation will face serious consequences for validating this atrocity and calling it *reproductive health care* and a *woman's right*.

Consequences to Ancient Israel

For David and the nation of Israel, different consequences arose from his murder of Uriah. Not only did that son die, causing heartache to David and Bathsheba, but other trouble followed. Read 2 Samuel 13:1–21. Since David had multiple wives, there were a lot of half-brothers and half-sisters in his household. This gave occasion for sinful lusts to emerge.

David's son Amnon thought he was in love with his half-sister, Tamar. On bad advice, he concocted a scheme whereby he could seduce her. David should have been wise enough to recognize that there was something fishy about Amnon's request for Tamar to come and cook for him. Amnon even spelled it out for David: "Please let my sister Tamar come and cook my favorite dish as I watch. Then I can eat it from her own hands" (2 Samuel 13:6 NLT).

However, David went along with this request and sent her. And Amnon watched her knead the cakes, no doubt his lust growing with every move she made. It would take time for them to bake, and Tamar stayed until they were done. She brought them to him only for him to refuse to eat (v. 9). He sent away all the other people and then requested that she bring the food into his chamber and feed him from her hand.

It doesn't take a genius to realize that if he's lying on the bed and she's supposed to feed him from her hand, she has to sit on the bed or very near it. His next suggestion followed naturally from this weirdness: "Come lie with me, my sister"

(v. 11 KJV). Her reaction in verses 12 and 13 shows that she was aware he wasn't talking about just having a nap together. She even suggests that he ask their father, because surely the king would grant a marriage between them.

But instead of doing things the right way, he raped her. And once he had spoiled her virginity and had his way with her, he hated her. Why? Because to look at her brought him face to face with his sin and guilt and shame. And he couldn't handle it. His father, the king, had never taught him about the righteousness of God, the grace and forgiveness of God, or the real meaning of love.

So he kicks her out, a defiled young woman whom no other man will want to marry. She has nowhere to go but to her brother Absalom's house. And he, of course, knew what had happened.

We read in verse 21 that David also heard of it and was very angry. But he did nothing about it. He did not chastise Amnon. He did not offer condolences to Tamar or apologize for his role in what happened. How could he? He, himself, had called a married woman, wife of one of his faithful men, to come to his bed. And he had murdered her husband.

Now, we know that he could have spoken out. He had been forgiven of those sins. They were behind him. His responsibility was to speak out and set this right in some way. But how often do we find ourselves not speaking out against sin, not counseling our children or friends to do what God's Word says—simply because we, at one time, did the wrong thing ourselves?

Personal guilt and shame is a great silencer. If we have sinned, we don't need any edict demanding our privatization of faith. It's very human for us to just stop speaking about God's love, righteousness, and forgiveness, out of embarrassment over our failure. That's why obedience to God from early in our lives is such an important thing. Admitting and confessing our failure is also important. When we acknowledge our sin, we are better able to speak of God's forgiveness.

Amnon's wrong definition of love (which had turned to hate), generated more hate as Absalom began to hate his half-brother Amnon. He concocts a scheme and invites David to join him and all the king's sons on a journey to the sheepshearers. Presumably, they were taking a flock of sheep to be shorn. David declines but allows all his other sons to go with Absalom.

Again, we could wonder what David was thinking. His personal shame clouded his judgment. Does that not happen to us?

Absalom directs his servants to kill Amnon, and they do so. The other sons flee. But word gets to David that all the sons are dead, and he is beside himself. Notice that the same man who gave that bad counsel to Amnon in 2 Samuel 13:5 now informs David of the truth—that only Amnon is dead because of what he did to Tamar.

The shame of one person's sin multiplies and brings grief to the whole family. Compounded over and over, the destruction spreads to the whole society. Absalom stayed in exile for three years (2 Samuel 13:37–38). We read in verse 39 that king David "longed to be reunited with his son Absalom" (NLT). However, he took no action. And we read in 2 Samuel 14:24 that when he finally sent for Absalom to return, he said, "Absalom may go to his own house, but he must never come into my presence" (NLT).

Absalom had plotted murder against a half-brother who had raped his sister. David had plotted murder against a faithful man whose wife he had seduced. What could he say to Absalom?

But David's action, no doubt fraught with shame, bred even more sin and destruction. Pardon without reconciliation can breed bitterness and contempt. Thus, when Absalom takes drastic measures to gain an invitation to see his father the king, the apparent reconciliation is a ruse. Read 2 Samuel 14:25–33. It wasn't long before Absalom sought to take the kingdom from his father, David. Chapters 15 through 18 of 2 Samuel give us the story of this rebellion.

Indeed, the society was harmed by this unchecked sin and shame that arose from the wrong definition of love, from the satisfaction of lust and the consequences of that sin, and from a tarnished testimony that produced shame and silence when others needed godly advice.

Our Responsibility to the Culture

In short, when we mislabel and wrongly define love, we create confusion and give sin an inroad because of our tarnished testimony. When we base our judgment and decisions on wrong definitions, we will accept sin as okay—or do and say nothing to correct it. We will allow it the upper hand and give it permission to run its course in our lives, our families, and our society.

Speaking the truth in love and living the truth in love require us to make a stand for God's righteousness. We cannot cave in to politically correct tolerance, which has become simply the acceptance and validation of sin. We cannot endorse our culture's new definitions of love, marriage, and intimacy.

Since God is both love and righteousness, it follows that real love is righteous. Thus, if a feeling, wrongly called love by misguided people, is contrary to righteousness, it is not real love. Not godly love. Likewise, condemning or hating misguided people is neither righteous nor loving. We must always be motivated by agape love.

Thus, in addition to exposing, confessing, and turning from sin, we are to

- let our light shine (Matthew 5:16);
- be salt and preserve the culture from decay as long as possible (Matthew 5:13);
- be living testimonies of goodness (Titus 2:7–8);
- show God's righteousness to everyone around us (Titus 2:12); and
- let our love be without hypocrisy (Romans 12:9).

New Testament Sin and Consequences

In the New Testament, we see an incident in the city of Corinth that needed correction. It involved a man having sex with his stepmother (his father's wife). The believers in Corinth boasted of their *love* for these two and of the working of the grace of God to allow this behavior. They mistook liberty for license to sin. They misconstrued grace for acceptance of sin.

Read what Paul tells them in 1 Corinthians 5:1–5:

> I can hardly believe the report about the sexual immorality going on among you—something that even pagans don't do. I am told that a man in your church is living in sin with his stepmother. You are so proud of yourselves, but you should be mourning in sorrow and shame. And you should remove this man from your fellowship. Even though I am not with you in person, I am with you in the Spirit. And as though I were there, I have already passed judgment on this man in the name of the Lord Jesus. You must call a meeting of the church. I will be present with you in spirit, and so will the power of our Lord Jesus. Then you must throw this man out and hand him over to Satan so that his sinful nature will be destroyed and he himself will be saved on the day the Lord returns. (NLT)

Some will say, "That's not being very loving." But it is better love than the attitude of silence, which would allow the sin to continue and spread, defiling many.

By God's grace, the incident didn't end there. Because the church judged his behavior as wrong, the man repented and stopped sinning that sin. And in 2 Corinthians 2:5–11, Paul tells the believers at Corinth to restore the man to fellowship. He says, in part,

> Most of you opposed him, and that was punishment enough. Now, however, it is time to forgive and comfort him. Otherwise he may be overcome by discouragement. So I urge you now to reaffirm your love for him. (vv. 6–8 NLT)

The instruction is to forgive, comfort, and confirm love, lest he be consumed with sorrow.

What would happen if we confessed a sin, being fully convicted about it, but we never felt forgiven or accepted back into fellowship? Wouldn't it eat away at us, hindering our growth?

Sharing Reconciliation

We need that forgiveness and restoration. We need to feel that we are not alone, that others also might have erred but have been forgiven, and that the wrongdoing is in the past, removed from us as far as the east from the west. We need to have the love of others confirmed to us. We all need to feel loved and accepted. A sense of belonging is important to our emotional health. That's what the apostle Paul is saying here, to make the repentant believer feel that sense of belonging, that acceptance, that love of God.

Imagine what could have happened in the way of reconciliation and peace had David confirmed his love to Absalom and showed forgiveness, restoring fellowship. Imagine the effect if he had judged Amnon's sin and required his repentance. Or if he had denied the original request, thus preserving Tamar's purity. But David's silence, born of shame and embarrassment, kept him from speaking the truth in love. And his continued silence reaped the havoc that his earlier sin had sowed.

His silence fed the darkness that fell over his throne. Likewise, our silence can feed the darkness of our culture.

Reflect Further

1. Think of Scriptures that define the ideal behavior of Christians. (Some examples are Romans 12:9–21; Philippians 2:14–16; and Titus 2:11–12.) List the words and phrases used to describe the godly behavior of believers. Are we free to redefine those terms? Or should we hold fast to the original definitions of the Greek words as they have been translated?

2. I remember learning in elementary school that Philadelphia has been called the "City of Brotherly Love." That's because the Greek word for *brotherly love* is *philadelphia*. That Greek word is used in Romans 12:10 and other verses. The instruction is to be "kindly affectionate to one another with brotherly love" (NKJV). Any concordance will reveal that *kindly affectionate* is the Greek word that describes affection for one's kindred or fondness for natural relatives. It is expanded to include brotherly love for fellow Christians as spiritual relatives in Christ. However, in a society where family relationships have broken down and many people lack natural affection, is this instruction outdated? Why or why not?

3. Paul writes in 2 Corinthians 7:8–10 concerning his strong words in that matter of incest mentioned in 1 Corinthians 5:1–2. He writes,

    > I am not sorry that I sent that severe letter to you, though I was sorry at first, for I know it was painful to you for a little while. Now I am glad I sent it, not because it hurt you, but because the pain caused you to repent and change your ways. It was the kind of sorrow God wants his people to have, so you were not harmed by us in any way. For the kind of sorrow God wants us to experience leads us away from sin and results in salvation. There's no regret for that kind of sorrow. But worldly sorrow, which lacks repentance, results in spiritual death. (2 Corinthians 7:8–10 NLT)

    What is "worldly sorrow"? How does it result in spiritual death? Can a person be sorry for wrong actions (or sorry he/she was caught) without truly repenting of sin? What does true repentance lead to?

4. What brings us to repentance? Must we see our action as *sin* before we can be wooed by the loving invitation to God's blessings? Can we tell people that their actions are sin, but do it in a loving way that encourages repentance? In other words, although what they have done is sin, can we assure them that they are an individual loved by God and important to us?

5. Read Colossians 1:3–4; 2 Thessalonians 1:3; and Philemon 1:4–5. In these Scriptures and many others, *faith* and *love* are connected. Is it necessary to believe the truth of the gospel in order to love others with *agape love*, which is God's kind of love for us? Explain.

6. If we are established in faith and love, can we expect additional wisdom and revelation of God's Word? See Ephesians 1:15–17.

7. Read Psalm 51:1–13 and describe repentance as David discusses it there. If God wants all to come to repentance—as Peter says in 2 Peter 3:9—what is our responsibility in bringing that to pass?

8. Read 2 Peter 3:18. If we grow in grace and knowledge, will we also grow in *agape* love? Explain.

CHAPTER 5

Our Silence Feeds the Darkness

As WE HAVE SEEN, our silence can feed the darkness, compounding our sin into multiple sins in our families, churches, and society. That's because when we are silent in the face of sin, we assent to that sin. We validate it, as it were. This keeps us from being persecuted or maligned for our stand for God's love, truth, and righteousness. But is that trade-off worthwhile?

Jesus warned the disciples about the persecution which would beset them. He warned them that the world would indeed hate them because it hates him (John 15:19). We've seen in the early chapters of Acts that both Jewish and Roman leaders hated the disciples. Those leaders hated the disciples just as they had hated Christ. Many of us feel that hatred against us today, though the ethnic group hating us is different.

The spirit that works in those who hate us is the spirit that works in the children of disobedience (Ephesians 2:2 KJV). That is the spirit of antichrist, of which we read in 1 John 4:3. It is the spirit that rejects Jesus as Son of God, born as a human to redeem fallen mankind and give eternal life to whosoever believes in him. It is the spirit that is in the world, the spirit of a culture in rebellion against God and God's order. The world calls it "social milieu" (French) or "zeitgeist" (German).

That spirit in the culture sees the Spirit of Truth in Christians and recoils from that light. The reason is simple. The Spirit of Truth convicts the world of its depravity and need. Let me say that again: the Spirit of Truth convicts the world of its depravity and need. God doesn't need us to speak it. The Holy Spirit is quite able to do so.

Regarding the Holy Spirit, Jesus says,

> And when he comes, he will convict the world of its sin, and of God's righteousness, and of the coming judgment. The world's sin is that it refuses to believe in me. Righteousness is available because I go to the Father, and you will see me no more. Judgment will come because the ruler of the world has already been judged. (John 16:8–11 NLT)

Unbelievers do not want to be reminded of their sin. If they acknowledge they have sin, then they must acknowledge they need the Savior and that they must repent of their sin. Repenting means turning away from the sin. That can't happen until they recognize it as sin. They refuse to call it sin because they do not want to cease and desist from their sinful activities.

Consequently, they deny the reality of sin, though our right living in Christ reminds them of it, by contrast. That's why they need us to accept their deeds as "not sin"—as "normal." If they can get us to concede that their choices are valid and right—that there is nothing wrong with their deeds, then they don't have to change their behavior. If they can get us to claim that God himself is okay with their behavior, then they don't have to admit their sin or face its consequences. And if we remain silent, they have won.

This is what the gay pride movement is all about, along with political correctness, tolerance, and the emergent gender confusion and "trans" movement. If we will celebrate gender diversity and inclusion with them, then their choices are validated. However, contrary to a popular social gospel, assenting to their sin does not soften them for the gospel. Rather, it hardens them to the truth and light of God's righteousness.

Blending in with them makes Christians appear no different than the world. And if we're no different, why be a Christian? A. W. Tozer said, "When we become so tolerant that we lead people into mental fog and spiritual darkness, we are not acting like Christians—we are acting like cowards."[1]

The Spirit of the World

The spirit of the world influences those in its grasp to deny basic physiology, science, and DNA evidence. They even reject the reality of body parts. And in January 2021, the House of Representatives introduced a bill to remove gender specific nouns and references from the language to be used in congress. Mother and father replaced by "parent"; grandma and grandpa replaced by "grandparent"; brother and sister replaced by "sibling"; and so on. Replacing "daughter-in-law" with "child-in-law" is an insult to my very mature daughter-in-law.

This denial and distortion of basic language compounds the secular culture's departure from science. The representatives even went so far as to disregard the meaning of the word "Amen." They chose to misinterpret it and compound their foolishness by adding an "Awoman," to the end of a so-called prayer. Thus, they showed their disdain of God, of Christians, and of prayer.

Recently, I saw a Facebook meme which showed the steps of decline that happen when we stop standing for biblical morality. In charting the downhill slide, I added a step to it along with the popular terms of our culture.

- First, we overlook evil, calling it "individual preference."
- Then we permit evil, claiming "tolerance."
- Then we legalize evil, declaring "freedom of choice."
- Then we promote evil in the name of "diversity."
- Then we celebrate evil and insist on conformity to "political correctness."
- Then we call evil good, professing "relative morality" and demanding "inclusion."
- Then we persecute those who still call it evil, alleging "social justice."

This is why we cannot be silent. When we stop preaching the gospel, stop telling people about the love of God in sending the Savior to rescue them from sin—when we stop sharing eternal life—the spirit of the world takes our culture down that slippery slope to judgment and woe.

Isaiah writes, "Woe to those who call evil good, and good evil; Who substitute darkness for light and light for darkness; Who substitute bitter for sweet and sweet for bitter!" (Isaiah 5:20 NASB). The Hebrew word translated "woe" is a statement like "alas!" and expresses grief, in the sense of crying out or lamentation.

Hence, the translation of that verse from the *New Living Translation*: "What sorrow for those who say that evil is good and good is evil, that dark is light and light is dark, that bitter is sweet and sweet is bitter."

But that's what happens when we back down from the truth and fail to share the gospel message—evil is called good, and good is called evil. That's how our culture became this dark. Christians kept their religion to themselves, so as not to offend anyone. We retreated from the public realm, from politics for the most part, and from Hollywood for a while (1980s and 1990s.)

Box Office History

In the 1950s, there were four popular box office hits dealing with the life and time of Jesus, three in the 1960s, and four in the 1970s, culminating with *The Jesus Film* in 1979, viewed by approximately 8.1 billion people (as of May 27, 2020). That film, used by Campus Crusade for Christ, has resulted in the salvation of an estimated 572 million people (as of May 27, 2020).[2]

Only one box office film about Jesus emerged from the 1980s. Blasphemous to the core, *Last Temptation of Christ* was poorly made. But it expressed the zeitgeist of the times. In contrast, the one film of this topic to come out of the 1990s was *Matthew*, well-made and faithful to the *New International Version* in the dialogue.

The 2000s saw three movies made about Christ, including Mel Gibson's *The Passion of the Christ*. This signals a change in the downward trend, as Christians re-entered Hollywood with a zeal to express truth and to counter the darkness that had all but consumed the entertainment industry.

Positive Influence of the "Code"

In his book *How to Succeed in Hollywood without Losing Your Soul*, Ted Baehr explains the changes in the entertainment industry. He tells how the movie industry was influenced positively by Christianity from 1933–1966, when the Motion Picture Code governed the box office screenings. That code upheld the dignity and sanctity of life. It limited profanity, obscenity, sexual activity, and acts of brutality and cruelty. It prohibited indecent exposure; words and symbols sparking bigotry or hatred; inhuman treatment of animals; justification of sin, crime, wrong-doing, or illicit sex; and the demeaning of religion.[3]

If you think back to those early days of film or watch old reruns, you'll agree with Baehr's assessment. He says, "For the most part, movies and television programs aligned with the biblical principles of communicating the true, the good, and the beautiful."[4]

But something went wrong. In 1966, "the churches voluntarily withdrew from the entertainment industry."[5] This upset the media elite and studio executives, who saw the church involvement as a positive influence on the box office. The Motion Picture Code was NOT censorship. It was patron sovereignty, which the moviemakers saw as the right of patrons to determine what they saw.[6]

One can wonder why the church left Hollywood. Was it in compliance to the growing spirit of the world? To the darkness which that spirit brought upon the culture? To the silencing of truth, goodness, and beauty?

Ongoing issues in 1965 and 1966 were, of course, the Civil Rights movement and race riots, with the calling in of National Guards; the Cold War and fears of nuclear aggression from the Soviet Union; the Space Race with a successful unmanned moon landing; and the Vietnam War, with its escalation and counter-culture war protests. Besides all this, the miniskirt came out in 1965, just one little indication of the loosening of the culture's moral fiber. In 1966, shifts in major movie studios occurred, and Walt Disney died. The original *Star Trek* series premiered.

You can easily Google for a full list of all major events of 1966. Here are some that reflect a change in the culture. Rebellion, unrest, open sexuality, and dissent marked the year as one of change.

- John Lennon of the Beatles claimed that they were more popular than Jesus. (He issued a reluctant and insincere apology later, when forced to do so.)
- The church of Satan was founded in San Francisco.
- Richard Speck murdered eight student nurses in their Chicago dormitory.
- Sniper Charles Whitman killed his wife and mother, and then went to the top of a university building in Austin, Texas, and killed thirteen people and wounded another thirty-one people.
- Investigations into anti-American activities by those aiding the Vietcong were disrupted by anti-war protesters.
- The daughter of a Republican candidate was stabbed and bludgeoned to death in the family home in Chicago.

Other things that occurred showed positive steps toward solving problems, or simply were sources of unrest and uncertainty of the times:

- Miranda Rights were instituted and the order given that they were to be recited before an arrest.
- The National Organization for Women (NOW) was founded as women's rights became an issue.
- At least two major airline crashes occurred in the states, claiming the lives of all on board.

- Sixteen were killed in Topeka, Kansas in an F5 tornado which destroyed much of the city.

I personally feel that the assassination of President Kennedy in 1963 was a major turning point in our culture. I know how it affected me, as a ninth grader. It was as though a switch flipped. Suddenly, what was certain and sure became unclear and unstable. If the president was not safe, no one was.

The foundation was no longer firm. Psalm 11:3 says, "If the foundations be destroyed, what can the righteous do?" (KJV). The *New Living Translation* states it more clearly: "The foundations of law and order have collapsed. What can the righteous do?" As when a building shakes in an earthquake and its inhabitants rush outside for safety, so did the church flee from Hollywood when they sensed the shaking and breaking of the foundations of morality, modesty, decency, and wholesomeness.

Christian Exodus from Hollywood

When the church retreated from Hollywood, "the Motion Picture Association of America (MPAA) instituted the rating system to take the place of the Code."[7] Today, the rating system can be used against faith-based films, giving "R" ratings to movies that oppose activities such as abortion, and giving "G" or "PG" ratings to movies that, in reality, should receive a rating of "R" or "X" because of their sexual content and blatant propaganda.

The groups that read the scripts, view the films, and rate the movies are often Marxist, feminist, or homosexual groups. Very few are given to Christian groups like Movieguide or Christian Film & Television Commission for rating.[8]

As a result, a great many television programs now feature gay characters and display affectionate gay relations, even during prime evening hours. Even commercials feature gays. One even encourages gay activities in spite of HIV infection. And we've all seen the way that many television shows and movies portray and denigrate Christians, even to the extent of mocking God.

Return to Hollywood

Fortunately, today there are a good number of Christian producers, directors, writers, and actors. The Christians have returned to Hollywood, often filming in other metropolitan film centers, like Austin, Atlanta, and in Canada. Faith-based films are making a comeback, and several have been top box office sensations.

I see this as the answer of Christians to the call to be light in a dark world. This response, better late than never, demonstrates why we cannot simply go away in silence. We must confront the darkness of our culture. We must stand up and hold forth the Word of Life. We must defend the reality of the gospel. We must find our voice and speak the truth in love.

However, we face an uphill battle, partly due to the influence of Hollywood. During the 70s, 80s, and 90s, much of what they produced showed an erroneous view of Christianity and Christians. Instead of presenting us as normal people with flaws but generally good intentions, they portrayed Christians as self-righteous hypocrites who spewed hatred and condemnation. They showed a critical and judgmental spirit as the motivation for believers in Christ.

This was a false view. But Hollywood was good at setting up this "straw man," so they could rightfully criticize it and tear it down. Even the original *Star Trek* challenged an often falsely portrayed Bible-based status quo.

Consequently, when the distorted view prevailed, part of the church answered by compromising righteousness and truth with political correctness and tolerance. We began to accept illicit relationships as real love. Another group began writing and producing cheesy movies that lacked a sense of reality. The rest of the church simply withdrew from Hollywood. The cultural darkness grew.

Standing against the Zeitgeist

By God's grace, a movement arose, however, where good movies began to be made. These had realistic situations and conflicts; true-to-life characters and problems; and good, solid writing, acting, and directing. Now, with the Kendrick brothers, David A.R. White, Chuck Konzelman, Cary Solomon, Kevin Sorbo, and other writers, directors, producers, and actors, the distorted view of Christians is being set right.

In 2019, a TV series *The Chosen* (2017), created by Dallas Jenkins, gained immediate success. Biblical history portrayed with excellence, it is the largest crowdfunded media project of all time (as of March 2021). The series is ranked 9.7 stars out of 10 on the well-known movie database site, *IMDb.com*. Many reviewers rave about its high quality.

And there are many other Christian moviemakers whose goal is to present the good, the true, and the beautiful in their films that are not specifically hailed as faith-based but are good, moral art from a Christian worldview.

Some of the Christian movies in recent years have become box office sensations, often outdoing secular movies. I'm sure each person has his or her favorite film. But we are locked in a battle for the culture. The spirit of darkness moves on secular moviemakers in their disparagement of the Lord, his gospel, and his people. And the Holy Spirit of truth prompts Christian moviemakers to present gospel truth beautifully, artistically, and with excellence.

First Century Straw Men

Straw man arguments were used in the first century church, as well. When the apostle Paul and his helpers first ministered at Philippi, a slave girl with a spirit of divination followed them around and actually announced that they were "the servants of the Most High God, who proclaim to us the way of salvation" (Acts 16:17 NKJV). Read Acts 16:18–34.

She did this many days. And though she spoke truth, Paul objected to having a pagan fortune-teller announcing their ministry. He discerned that she spoke by means of a demonic spirit. So, he simply cast the demon out of her. When she no longer could profit her owners, they ganged up on Paul and Silas and hauled them to court. Of course, they falsely accused them of stirring up trouble in the city and inciting the people to keep unlawful customs. After severely beating Paul and Silas, they threw them into an inner prison, fastening their feet in stocks.

Now, if Paul and Silas were guilty of those crimes, they belonged in prison. But they were not guilty. The charges were another straw man designed to make them look worthy of judgment. But at midnight, "Paul and Silas prayed, and sang praises unto God: and the prisoners heard them" (v. 25 KJV).

You can read how God intervened with an earthquake that loosed the chains of all the prisoners, and how the jailer, when he awoke, sought to kill himself, supposing they had escaped and he would be executed for sleeping on the job and letting them get away. Paul stopped him, crying out, "Do yourself no harm, for we are all here" (v. 28 NKJV).

The jailer "called for a light" (v. 29 NKJV). I love that. Yes, he wanted to see for himself that they were indeed all there. He called for a light—and Jesus is the true Light that shines in the darkness. The jailer received a light—and then he received the Light (vv. 31–34). And not only the jailer. He asked how he could be saved, and Paul answered: "Believe in the Lord Jesus and you will be saved, along with everyone in your household" (v. 31 NLT).

His household came to faith, were all baptized, and ministered to Paul and Silas.

Silence and Compromise Are Not the Answer

Imagine how different the outcome would have been if Paul and Silas had just kept silent. Imagine if they had said in response to the accusations, "Oh, my. We're sorry we offended you. We'll stop preaching. We don't want you to feel bad." Or if they'd told the jailer, "Well, we're sure you are sincere in what you believe, so you probably will be saved. I mean, it's all you know, so culturally you can't be expected to believe what we believe."

We can see how silly these alternate messages would have been. And yet, how do we respond to slander or rejection from the world? How would we respond to praise or recognition by unbelievers? How do we answer the straw man charges against us? How do we answer the sincere questions that some people might ask regarding how to be saved? Can we answer with boldness and love, as did Paul and Silas?

We dare not compromise, back down, or step aside. We cannot go to the closet. As a body, we have done that to the detriment of our culture and to the endangerment of our children and grandchildren.

We must stand—and having done all—continue to stand. Not in haughtiness. Not as holier-than-thou. Not in anger or retaliation. We stand in obedience to Christ and in love for all, for both those who stand with us and those who stand against us.

Reflect Further

1. Read Matthew 10:32–33; Mark 8:38; Luke 9:26; and 2 Timothy 2:12–13. Note Jesus' words about denying those who deny him. Does this mean that believers who deny him in the face of a hostile culture will lose their salvation? Did Peter, after he denied Jesus three times? No. But eternal rewards are at stake. In 2 Timothy 2:12, Paul makes it clear that if we deny the Lord the opportunity to bring us through persecution and suffering, then he will deny us the privilege and reward of ruling and reigning with him. We will have a lower place in heaven than one of reigning. Verse 13 declares his guarantee: "If we are faithless, He remains faithful; He cannot deny Himself" (NKJV). So who are they who deny Jesus and are then denied by him?

2. Do you see an apt description of our time in Mark 8:38? What does it mean that Jesus would be "ashamed of" believers who allow the culture to bully them into being ashamed of him and his Word?

3. Read Luke 9:23–25. What does it mean to deny self and take up one's cross daily? Should we allow a certain segment in our culture to bankrupt us and ruin our businesses rather than compromise with and validate their behavior?

4. Read Psalm 41:5–11; 109:20, 29–31; Matthew 5:44; and Luke 6:28. In the Old Testament, the psalmist could ask for judgment on his enemies who lied about him. Is that what we are to do today? What should our attitude be?

5. Should we take it personally when secular people slander us? Should we fear them? Should we compromise so they won't think those things of us? If we remain true to the Lord and his Word, will we come out on top? Even if we face persecution and death?

6. Those who speak evil of us also speak evil of God and his Word. Do you see this effect in our culture? As we pray for them, can we also stand for truth, goodness, and beauty? How?

7. There are places in the world today where Christians are killed for their faith. Nigeria is one of those places. Others are countries in the Mideast and many in Asia, such as Indonesia, North Korea, and China. These are known to not be safe for Christians. Would you be able to stand against that persecution as Christians there do? Do you think that will ever be the situation in the United States?

CHAPTER 6

Speaking the Truth in Love

WHEN WE STAND FOR TRUTH, we must stand in love. The truth, stripped of love, grace, and mercy, is simply judgment, however righteous it may be. To speak truth is important, but it must be spoken in love.

When the woman who was taken in adultery was brought before Jesus, those Pharisees who brought her spoke truth that she had committed a sin punishable by death (John 8:1–12). Jesus knew the truth of the law. But he tempered his knowledge of truth with his love and grace. He challenged them that the one without sin should cast the first stone. Another truth for them to take into account. They had to acknowledge the scriptural principle of Psalm 14:1–3, which Paul draws from in Romans 3:10: "There is none righteous, no, not one" (NKJV).

And then he simply wrote on the ground. And as they read what he wrote, they were convicted of their own sins and had to depart. Can't you hear those stones dropping to the sand, one after another? Thud. Thud. Thud. And the retreating footsteps of the Pharisees until none were left in that circle of judgment around her. Then Jesus asks, "Where are your accusers? Did no one condemn you?" (John 8:10 MEV).

He knew they stepped away because they had sin, but he was making a point.

We see from verse 13 that they were still nearby, near enough to hear him. After all, they were trying to test him. Either way, they thought they had him. If he didn't stone her, they could accuse him of not upholding the law. If he did stone her, they could claim that her blood was upon him. After all, how would his followers take this in light of all his other teachings?

Though the Pharisees denied it, Jesus was the only one without sin. It was his right to pick up a stone and hurl it at her. Stone after stone after stone. But he did not do that. He who gave the law to Moses seemed to set it aside. He knew a greater law was here, and a greater man than Moses.

There are some who think he let her off too lightly. However, he did not pronounce her adultery okay or say that he'd overlook it this time. He didn't announce that God had relaxed his standards of righteousness and the law no longer applied. He didn't declare that the law was outdated or old fashioned, so he wasn't going to judge her. He didn't excuse her because of special circumstances or because of relative morality in the culture. He didn't assert her right to choose who her bed partners would be.

No. What he said was this: "Neither do I condemn you; go and sin no more" (John 8:11 NKJV). He refused to condemn her. He set her free—"go." And he instructed her to stop sinning. No easy task.

Often, we stop reading there. But verse 12 is the key to his instruction to her and his explanation to the Pharisees and to his followers: "Jesus spoke to the people once more and said, 'I am the light of the world. If you follow me, you won't have to walk in darkness, because you will have the light that leads to life'" (NLT).

The True Light

John 1:9 states that Jesus is the true Light. When we read his words in John 3:18–21, we see a marvelous truth about our response to that true light.

> He who believes in Him is not condemned; but he who does not believe is condemned already, because he has not believed in the name of the only begotten Son of God. And this is the condemnation, that the light has come into the world, and men loved darkness rather than light, because their deeds were evil. For everyone practicing evil hates the light and does not come to the light, lest his deeds should be exposed. But he who does the truth comes to the light, that his deeds may be clearly seen, that they have been done in God. (NKJV)

The reason Jesus did not condemn the woman taken in adultery is that she was condemned already. Being condemned is the condition in which we all start. The only way to become not condemned is to come to the light, which Jesus is. To believe in him. Furthermore, the way to stop sinning is to follow Jesus, as he says in John 8:12, so that we no longer walk in darkness. This is the message of truth which Jesus spoke to that woman and to all who were listening. And he spoke it with love.

Still True Today

That message still holds true today. Accepting Jesus as our Savior and Lord gives us "the light of life" and enables us to walk in that light, not in the darkness of our former sins. Receiving the true Light moves us from condemnation to not being condemned.

Of course, if we break the law of a human government, we don't get off that easily before the world. Peter mentions this in 1 Peter 4:15 when he cautions the believers against actions that would lead to their punishment as wrongdoers. If we do wrong, we will most likely suffer the consequences of our actions. If we then receive Jesus and walk in the light, he will not condemn us. Though forgiven by God, we will still face the results and penalties for wrongdoing.

If we already have received him, but then commit a crime, we will still face the consequences of the judgment by the world. And that would be just. However, our standing before God is that we are *not condemned* because we have come to the light of Jesus Christ. Of course, God prefers that we don't sin but that we would walk in the light of Jesus.

Hence, Jesus urged the woman taken in adultery, "Go and sin no more." He has given us the power to sin no more—to walk in the light and follow him. And when we share this message with others, framed in the love in which Jesus spoke the message, we will be able to stand in the face of rejection, persecution, and hatred, just as Jesus did.

How Do We Speak in Love?

It might seem easy to speak with love toward someone who actually repents and wants a changed life. I'm pretty sure that Jesus knew the heart of that woman that day. He knew her desperation, not only to avoid being stoned to death, but her deeper desperation as she searched for love "in all the wrong places." He knew what her heart longed for. And he knew how to fill that need. He filled it with himself.

Every heart has a void that can only be filled by the true and living God. But some people harden their hearts and refuse to receive God. How do we speak the truth in love to them? How do we shine light into their chosen darkness?

How did Jesus do it in the presence of the Pharisees? He proclaimed who he is and what the benefit of following him would be to them. Did they accept that? No. Read John 8:13–19. His proclamation became even more pointed. They understood what he was saying. They knew that he claimed to be the Son of God. Furthermore, they saw the proofs that the God whom they professed to worship was truly his Father.

In John 8:21–24, he continues the conversation, letting them know that they are of the world but he is not. He even tells them that they will die in their sins if they refuse to believe who he is. So they ask him who he is (v. 25). At first they don't understand his answer (v. 27). Does Jesus give up? No.

He speaks to them about his coming crucifixion and the power behind his words and deeds—his Father in heaven. Praise God for verse 30: "As He said these things, many came to believe in Him" (NASB).

In verses 31–32, he encourages the believing Jews to continue in his word, "and you will know the truth, and the truth will set you free" (v. 32 NASB).

The Jews who did not believe continued to argue with him, verses 33–57. Because they rejected his divine nature implanted in Mary, they called him a product of fornication. They called him a Samaritan, because he grew up in Nazareth. They accused him of being demon possessed—a serious blasphemy.

When he claimed the name of God that they understood to be the "I AM" of Exodus 3:14, they picked up stones to stone him (yes, those very same stones they dropped at the beginning of this discourse). But it wasn't his time or method of death, so he "hid Himself and went out of the temple. Going through their midst, He passed by" (John 8:59 MEV).

Was he speaking the truth in love? Yes. Of course. He greatly desired their salvation. But part of speaking the truth in love is to say those things which convict of sin and point out need, in addition to setting forth what meets the need and removes sin. Sometimes speaking the truth in love requires stern language.

Different Approaches for Different Folks

This is why Jude writes of different tactics for different people in verses 22–23 of his letter: "And you must show mercy to those whose faith is wavering. Rescue others by snatching them from the flames of judgment. Show mercy on still others, but do so with great caution, hating the sins that contaminate their lives" (NLT).

There are some whom we are to encourage and remind of their salvation and of God's faithfulness. There are others with whom we need to be bold, telling them that they are sinning, that they need Jesus in order to go to heaven, and that if they reject him, they will face eternity in the flames of hell. Others, we are to be merciful to, but careful that we do not become defiled by or a party to their sin.

I think of this category when I think of ministering to those caught up in the LGBTQ lifestyle. We ought to show them mercy. Many of them truly are confused about their sexuality, their identity, and their emotions. They can feel as "in love" as heterosexual couples. And if they endure a breakup with their partner, the emotional pain can be as great as in a broken heterosexual relationship. We need compassion in ministering to them.

However, we cannot let our sympathy for them overshadow the message of the gospel, that coming to the light, which Jesus is, involves acknowledgment of sin, a desire to change, and a new birth which brings that change. "This means that anyone who belongs to Christ has become a new person. The old life is gone; a new life has begun!" (2 Corinthians 5:17 NLT).

We can't compromise and tell them that their homosexual relationships are okay with God. We cannot call those relationships normal. And we should not celebrate their chosen lifestyle by participating in their weddings or other life events that applaud their sin. We dare not commend their adoption of children or their use of an outsider to conceive a baby. We must guard against being sucked into their sin under a false pretense of showing love. In this case, love pronounces sin for what it is and points the way to the Savior. Love without truth isn't real love.

The same principle applies to abortion. Though we may sympathize with a woman regarding the circumstances of her pregnancy, we dare not tell her that abortion is okay. We cannot accept the willful ending of an innocent life as simply a "choice" the mother can make or a "right" that she has. And definitely we must oppose the making of that choice at full term, as some states now allow and encourage.

Does God forgive those who abort? Yes, when they are born-again. Does he accept abortion as a valid choice? No. He regards it as infanticide and idolatry, as much as the ancient worship of Molech was. In that heathen religion, mothers would lay their babies and small children in the arms of an idol. The idols had a place for fire within them—a fire that heated the bronze arms into which the mothers laid their children.

We shudder at that and think, "How barbaric!" And yet, what do we call the dismembering of infants in the womb? The scalding of infants in the womb with a potent saline solution? The poisoning of a very tiny baby, barely conceived (scientifically called a zygote), with a "morning-after" pill? A partial-birth abortion, where delivery of the baby starts, but then the child's spinal cord is severed from the brain before the birth is completed?

Can we call it "choice"? No. We must call it what it is. But we should do so in love, pointing mothers to the cross, where sin is forgiven and new life begins.

Can't we just ignore the topic? After all, we don't have the right to tell others how to live.

Look at what has happened to our society when we did ignore these sins. A quote often attributed to Dietrich Bonhoeffer appears regularly as a Facebook meme. It says, "Silence in the face of evil is itself evil: God will not hold us guiltless. Not to speak is to speak. Not to act is to act."[1] Whether it is Bonhoeffer's exact words or those of another, it is a true statement. One we do well to heed.

Silence Is Agreement

When I was in high school debate class, we had an expression for those moments when our opponent failed to address one or more of our points: "I take my opponent's silence as concurrence to this point." If we refuse to speak against sin, we are consenting to it and agreeing with it. If we fail to take action against evil, we have sided with evil.

We may remain silent or speak the truth in love. Our choice. Either way, our voice will proclaim our stand—for sin or against sin; with evil or with Christ; in darkness or in light.

How to Speak the Truth in Love

"Speaking the truth in love" involves a delicate balance between love and truth. Second John 1:3 provides that balance. John writes, "Grace, mercy, and peace, which come from God the Father and from Jesus Christ—the Son of the Father—will continue to be with us who live in truth and love" (NLT). Grace, mercy, and peace accompany truth and love. We do receive grace, mercy, and peace when we embrace God's truth and convey his love.

In fact, our receipt of God's grace, mercy, and peace enables us to communicate his love to others. But a message of love without a message of truth will bring neither peace nor mercy nor grace. The truth that Jesus Christ is Lord, Son of the Father, and Light of the World is an essential truth. One must embrace that truth to receive salvation by grace through faith. One must cling to that truth to receive the God of love and the love of God.

God's desire is for all believers to grow up in Christ. We see this in Ephesians 4:11–16. We are to grow up so that we won't be children, easily misled by deceitful people in the world, "But speaking the truth in love, may grow up into him in all things, which is the head, even Christ" (v. 15 KJV). But to whom are we to speak the truth in love?

To all. We saw some specific categories in the verses from Jude. Paul gives a general instruction in Colossians 4:6: "Let your speech always be with grace, seasoned with salt, that you may know how you should answer everyone" (MEV). When things are seasoned with salt, they are appealing, attractive, tasty, and delicious, for the most part. I know some of us have to observe a low-salt diet, but even with a salt substitute or herbs, sometimes I just hunger for the taste of sodium chloride—table salt.

Salt—the truth—is that which seasons the message of love. Together with grace, it makes the message appetizing, palatable, and pleasant. Moreover, grace and truth enable us to answer everyone. In that verse, "answer" means "to respond to." The Greek word corresponds to a Hebrew word meaning "testify; give account."

Does this imply that we all are to be preachers, prepared with sermons everywhere we go? No. But as redeemed individuals, we ought always to be ready to explain salvation, to share our story, and to introduce people to Jesus.

Always Be Ready to Speak

Peter wrote in his letter a similar instruction: "Instead, you must worship Christ as Lord of your life. And if someone asks about your hope as a believer, always be ready to explain it. But do this in a gentle and respectful way. Keep your conscience clear" (1 Peter 3:15–16 NLT).

Since Peter wrote to individual believers, we can safely conclude that ordinary folks like us must be prepared to share the gospel with anyone who asks or shows an interest in hearing it. At the very least, we should be prepared to tell how it has changed and influenced our lives.

Does that mean we must only speak when someone asks? Wouldn't that be the "polite" way? And we could leave all that other evangelizing to the preachers. After all, it's their job.

The fact is that our mouths will speak something. We will either discuss trivial things like the weather; personal things like our family, kids' accomplishments, or health issues; or political arguments and conspiracies. Or we can talk about Jesus, who enables us to deal with all those other things.

Paul tells us that we will reap what we sow (Galatians 6:7–9). Therefore, we will reap only temporal fruit, if any, from discussing weather, family, or politics. Sometimes those discussions will reap envy or anger. But if we sow the word of God, we'll reap eternal fruit—even if the person does not respond to God's Word in our presence.

Words as Seeds

The Bible often speaks of giving out the word as "sowing seed." A number of parables feature this. One in particular is found in three of the gospel records. You can read it in Matthew 13:3–8, 18–23; Mark 4:3–9, 14–20; and Luke 8:5–8, 11–15. It is the parable of the four types of soil. The seed is the Word of God, which the sower sows (Luke 8:11).

This sower was not really a professional farmer. He wasn't careful about where he sowed the seeds. Everywhere he happened to be, he let some seed fall. In the realm of farming, we could say that he had no agriculture degree, no family coaching, no fancy planter or seed driller. He was like regular Christians. No D. D. degree. No master degree in theology. No fancy recording equipment or website. Just a person sowing seed.

The seed that fell by the wayside was bird food before it could sprout. Have you ever witnessed to someone and really thought they understood and wanted to believe, but the next time you saw them, they were more opposed than ever to the gospel? These are the ones from whom Satan steals the word before it can take root in their hearts (Mark 4:15). It's not your fault. It's their choice. Keep praying for them. Keep sowing as the Holy Spirit prompts. Perhaps they'll yet embrace the Word.

Some seed fell on stony ground and quickly sprouted in the one inch of soil atop the rocks. What quick results! Alas, the noon sun scorched it, and it withered. Mark 4:16–17 explains who these are. Have you ever known people like that? They were so excited about the Lord at first. Perhaps they loved to worship and sing. Maybe they were drawn to meetings where healings occurred. They looked for miracles. But, in the absence of sound teaching, they didn't grow deep into the Lord and his Word. They didn't lose their salvation. They merely lost the assurance and joy of salvation. They need a dose of plant food, water, and good light. Spiritually that is nourishment from the Word; Water of the Word, which is a symbol for the Holy Spirit; and the light of life, which is Jesus.

Thirdly, some seed fell among thorns. The seeds sprouted and grew. But the thorns and weeds choked it out. They stunted its growth so that it didn't bloom or bear any fruit. I've been known to let the grass and weeds overtake areas of my garden in late summer. Then I'm angry at myself for wasting the opportunity for an abundance of late summer tomatoes.

We can see in Mark 4:18–19 what the thorns represent. The cares of this life—all those distracting things like bills, car breakdowns, property taxes due, difficulties on the job, a family crisis, and so on. And if we have enough money to not worry about those things, then the gaining and keeping of wealth—the stock market roller coaster—can sidetrack us. And if we aren't concerned about money, then other things we might desire—other priorities—can stunt our growth.

When we share Jesus with others and see that their lives are so full of extraneous drama, we can see this type of soil.

Again, it's not our fault. But it is our responsibility to speak to them in love, to encourage them to pull out those weeds and thorns and to focus on Jesus. And we need to uproot our own weeds too.

Finally, the seed sown on good ground bears fruit in varying degrees. If you plant gardens, you know that sometimes one tomato plant will outperform all the others. Sometimes a plant will only produce a few tomatoes in comparison, but they will taste delicious. The key is to plant in good, rich soil; continue to feed and water the plants; and keep the weeds out.

Another parable about sowing seed is in Matthew 13:24–30, 37–43. In this story, one man sows good seed in a field. Then, at night, his enemy comes and sows weeds in that field, and not just any weed but a weed that looks like the good plant. The farmer knows he must wait until mature grain appears on the good plants. Then he can send reapers to pull up and burn the weeds, which are the plants without grain. Then they can harvest the wheat.

Though this has an application to end time judgment, and the seed represents people, we can see it as a lesson about our witnessing right now. We sow the good seed—the Word of God. The world sows weeds—competing values, secular worldviews, and warped morals.

Spiritually speaking, the Lord knows when he has prepared hearts to receive the Word. He knows the seed that needs to be spoken. He knows the weeds we must root out. When he leads us to speak, we must be bold to speak the truth in love, to proclaim the gospel, and to share our testimony as an example of God's love.

And we need to follow God's leading, whether people listen or whether they scoff at us and bully us. Their response should not govern our obedience to God. Our faith and his love should govern our voice.

Reflect Further

1. Read Psalm 126:5–6; Galatians 6:7–9; and 1 Corinthians 3:6–9. Though sowing and reaping refers, as we saw in the parable, to giving out the Word to various people in different situations, can it represent more? What are some of the things it can represent?

2. What does Psalm 126:6 mean when it says those who sow with tears will reap with joy? Who are the tears for?

3. Read Mark 4:26–29. Does this parable refer to what we sow in our lives? When will our fruit be mature, and, thus, ready to be harvested?

4. When we sow the Word—share it with others—can we trust it to grow and bring forth fruit under the watchful care of God? What are other pertinent elements of the parable in Mark 4?

5. Referring to 1 Corinthians 3:6–9, think of a time in your life when one person planted and another watered? Were the planter and waterer aware of each other? Do we need to be? Why or why not?

6. Read Exodus 4:10–12; Jeremiah 1:7–9; Matthew 10:19–20; Mark 13:11; and Luke 12:11–12. God promises to give prophets and disciples the right words to speak. Is his

promise only for important Bible people? Is it only for the end times? Or can we trust the Holy Spirit to lead us NOW and give us words to speak to a hurting world and a dark culture?

7. What if we think not in terms of the world or culture, but in terms of one person whom God has placed in our path at this moment? Can we trust God to give us the right words to say?

8. Read Luke 21:12–15. Will the words God gives us be enough for the situation?

9. If we know a person's struggle, we may know how to address it from our own experience. If we aren't personally acquainted with them and we know only that they need the Lord, can we trust the Holy Spirit to give us words to reach them with the gospel?

10. Can we pick up on their comments or questions and start there—giving an answer by sharing our own testimony with them and pointing them to Christ who rescued and redeemed us?

11. What happens if we just remain silent?

CHAPTER 7

Love in Response to Bullies

KNOWING A PERSON'S STRUGGLE and having compassion for them is integral to speaking the truth in love. In our culture, where natural affection is dying and understanding others is absent, the phenomenon of bullying has risen to the forefront. We hear about it almost daily. Often, *being bullied* is given as the motivational force behind school shooters or child suicide victims. It is very real and very painful for our youth to endure. *Bullying* has become more vicious than in my childhood days when it was simply verbal taunting or the playing of pranks. Among adults, it can manifest as *racial profiling* in some—but not all—law enforcement personnel.

On the other hand, our culture seems to increasingly bully Christians. Several mayors and governors have launched campaigns against our holding church services, worshipping with song in limited meetings, or even having drive-in services. Some people expect that to change after wide-spread vaccinations are completed since the bullies use Covid-19 as their excuse or justification.

Additionally, we read of research that claims to have found a genetic anomaly in Christians that makes us violent.

We're even accused of being domestic terrorists. Some of our accusers support non-Christian groups that riot, burn, loot, and destroy lives and properties of select neighborhoods.

This new kind of bullying is not easily ignored or dealt with.

In Canada, the bullying has gone over the top. In April 2021, Grace Life Church in Alberta was closed, its pastor jailed, and a double fence erected around the building and grounds. An eight foot fence surrounded the parking lot. Inside that, another eight foot fence surrounded the building and was covered with privacy cloth.

This black cloth suggested that something insidious was planned by the government for that church building—something they didn't want people to see. Several agencies, the RCMP, and at least one private security company blocked all access to the grounds, both with vehicle blockades and police presence. Will the same thing happen in the USA?

Those of us who are over fifty can look back at bullying or being bullied in our youth. We were taught either to ignore the bully or fight back if the bullying was physical. I remember being verbally taunted because I wore glasses and orthopedic shoes. Consequently, I learned to tease others, which I deeply regret today. Bullying is old creation behavior and not pleasing to God. It arises from envy, jealousy, false pride, insecurity, or fear.

Bullying in Ancient Times

We can look back at Genesis and see bullying in action. Think of Joseph, favorite son of Jacob. This young lad knew the God of Abraham and Isaac and Jacob. He knew that their God was his God, too. He even received prophetic dreams from God. Dreams that he eagerly shared with his brothers and father. We can read about them in Genesis 37.

Was he boasting? From their perspective, yes. They already hated him because their father favored him and gave him a special coat of many colors. When he told them his dream—one that suggested he would reign over them—they hated him even more.

Then he dreams another dream and tells even his father, who rebukes him: "What is this dream that you have had? Am I and your mother and your brothers actually going to come to bow down to the ground before you?" (Genesis 37:10 NASB).

Maybe those dreams were something Joseph should have kept silent about. But from his perspective, he was sharing what he believed were dreams from God. And they were, in fact. Was it pride that caused him to speak out? We can't judge his heart, but we do know that his dreams caused his brothers to hate and envy him and caused his father to take note of those dreams (v. 11). But that response on their part does not mean that he should not have spoken about them.

As the story unfolds, we see his brothers putting him in a pit and selling him into slavery. Nine of them wanted to kill him, but Reuben spoke up with the pit idea. Reuben planned to rescue him and send him home to their father.

However, before he could do so and while he was apparently not present, Judah came up with the idea to sell Joseph to the Ishmaelites who sold him to the Midianites who sold him into Egypt to one of Pharaoh's officers, a captain of the guard.

We can read more of the consequences of the brothers' treatment of Joseph in Genesis 39 and 40. If anyone ever had a right to be angry with his brothers and to seek revenge, Joseph was such a man. By the time he finally gets out of prison (Genesis 41), he has not only suffered for things he did not do, but he also has had the emotional trauma of not seeing his father again—of not even having a chance to let his father know where he was and how he got there.

When Pharaoh calls on Joseph to interpret his dream, Joseph answers humbly, "It is not in me. God will give Pharaoh a favorable answer" (Genesis 41:16 MEV). Once Joseph interprets the dream and tells Pharaoh what to do in response to it, Pharaoh makes him the highest authority in the land, second only to Pharaoh himself.

Thus, Joseph's own dreams from his youth begin coming to pass. We see this in great detail in Genesis 42—50. When his brothers who come to Egypt for food in the time of famine bow before him in fear, he announces that he is their brother and says:

> Now do not be grieved or angry with yourselves because you sold me here, for God sent me ahead of you to save lives. . . . God sent me ahead of you to ensure for you a remnant on the earth, and to keep you alive by a great deliverance. Now, therefore, it was not you who sent me here, but God; and He has made me a father to Pharaoh and lord of all his household, and ruler over all the land of Egypt. (Genesis 45:5, 7–8 NASB)

Eventually the whole family comes down to Egypt. When Jacob dies, Joseph and his brothers take his body to the land of Israel to bury him. But when they return to Egypt, the brothers are worried that, now that dad is gone, Joseph will take his revenge. We read,

> Then his brothers also came and fell down before him and said, "Behold, we are your servants." But Joseph said to them, "Do not be afraid, for am I in God's place? As for you, you meant evil against me, but God meant it for good in order to bring about this present result, to keep many people alive. (Genesis 50:18–20 NASB)

To make that statement required an attitude of forgiveness and love, mercy and grace. It required an assurance that God was in complete control.

How We Should Handle Being Bullied

When we face intimidation and maltreatment for speaking the truth, can we take this same attitude—in love—that God is in control, allowing the actions against us and sovereignly working them for our good? We do know that he works all things together "for good to them that love God, to them who are the called according to his purpose" (Romans 8:28 KJV). But do the "all things" include harassment, oppression, bullying, and persecution?

Yes, they do. And yes, we can, as we trust in the Lord and rely upon the Holy Spirit. Stephen did, as we saw in Acts 7. He was badgered and tortured to death. His tormentors even gnashed on him with their teeth. They hurled stones at him until he was dead from the bruising and bashing of soft tissue (and probably the fracturing of bones). And with his dying breath he prayed, "Lord, lay not this sin to their charge" (Acts 7:60 KJV). That took love and forgiveness.

Paul, who was hounded and vexed during his entire ministry, stated in regard to those who oppressed him: "My heart is filled with bitter sorrow and unending grief for my people, my Jewish brothers and sisters. I would be willing to be forever cursed—cut off from Christ!—if that would save them (Romans 9:2-3 NLT). He was willing to be condemned if, by that, the Jews could be saved. That took love and forgiveness.

Of course, salvation doesn't work that way. But that was his heart's expression of the sacrificial love he felt for those who persecuted him. We can see some of the oppression he faced in Acts 14:1–7, 19–20; 17:5, 13; 18:12; 21:27–36. And Paul still wanted to see their lives changed (Acts 21:37—22:23).

Paul suffered persecution at the hands of the non-Jewish world, also. We can see this in Acts 16:19–24 and 19:34–41. And he held the same attitude of love and forgiveness toward the Gentiles. See what he says about them in Acts 28:28: "Therefore let it be known to you that the salvation of God has been sent to the Gentiles, and they will hear it!" (NKJV). A major part of his ministry was preaching Jesus to the Gentiles (non-Jews). See also Galatians 3:14; Ephesians 2:11–22; 3:6–8; and Colossians 1:27.

How we respond to oppression, harassment, intimidation, and persecution is a major factor in our witnessing to the world. We can speak the truth in love, but what really sets us apart from the world is how we respond if and when that truth is rejected. When people who reject Christ also reject us, how should we respond?

Forgiveness is the Key

Jesus and his follower, Stephen, forgave those who killed them. Joseph forgave those of his own family who sold him into slavery. David forgave King Saul, who tried to kill him several times, and he provided for Saul's descendants. (See 1 Samuel 18:9–11; 19:9–18; and 2 Samuel 9:1–13.)

One can read *Foxe's Book of Martyrs* to see how, through the centuries of persecution, committed Christians responded to persecution—even martyrdom. It is heavy reading. The types of physical torture that unbelievers and false believers inflicted on true Christians will make the hair on your neck bristle. It shows the reality of Paul's words in Romans 8:36 as he quoted Psalm 44:22: "For your sake we are killed every day; we are being slaughtered like sheep" (NLT).

I used to read that verse and think that it applied only to then, not now. Yet what do we see in the world today?

Global Persecution

Nigerian Christians (especially in the northern part of Nigeria) are some of the most persecuted Christians in the world today. I have seen so many cries go out to pray for the suffering church in Nigeria. And yet, those persecuted believers will ask prayer for the Muslim terrorists who are raping, kidnapping, and killing them, burning and pillaging their homes and churches, and stealing their property.

Christians in Indochina are being persecuted by Muslims. Christians in China are being persecuted by the Chinese government. North Korean Christians must hide their faith, lest they be killed. In India, Christians are often persecuted. Christians are slain in most Mideast countries that are controlled by Muslims, as well as many places in Africa.

We are challenged to look beyond our national borders at what our brothers and sisters in Christ are enduring TODAY, in this twenty-first century. And the demonically-controlled globalist movement that calls itself the New World Order will only make the persecution worse. It is coming to the USA.

We should not be surprised at this. It is prophesied. Jesus warned us of it as being what would follow the "beginning of sorrows" (Matthew 24:8 NKJV). We now see the things spoken of in Matthew 24:6–7 regarding that time: "Wars and rumors of wars . . . nation will rise against nation, and kingdom against kingdom. And there will be famines, pestilences, and earthquakes in various places" (NKJV).

But it doesn't stop there. Following those signs, Jesus said,

> "Then you will be arrested, persecuted, and killed. You will
> be hated all over the world because you are my followers.
> And many will turn away from me and betray and hate
> each other. And many false prophets will appear and will
> deceive many people. Sin will be rampant everywhere, and
> the love of many will grow cold." (Matthew 24:9–12 NLT)

This will be most obvious during the tribulation, after believers are raptured out, but it will also be obvious in the months or years leading up to the tribulation.

Notice that Christians would be hated "all over the world." The number of nations turning against the Christian faith is increasing. You can read reports of this persecution at persecution.com and persecution.org.

If the political party in the USA which has voted to remove God from its platform ever has control of all branches of government simultaneously (which it apparently does in 2021), you can be sure that the USA will join the ranks of those nations who hate and persecute Christians. Should this scare us? No. Look what Paul says next in Romans 8:37–39:

> No, despite all these things, overwhelming victory is ours
> through Christ, who loved us. And I am convinced that
> nothing can ever separate us from God's love. Neither
> death nor life, neither angels nor demons, neither our fears
> for today nor our worries about tomorrow—not even the
> powers of hell can separate us from God's love. No power
> in the sky above or in the earth below—indeed, nothing in
> all creation will ever be able to separate us from the love of
> God that is revealed in Christ Jesus our Lord. (NLT)

Persecuted, martyred, or surviving—"overwhelming victory is ours" or, as the *King James Version* translates verse 37, "we are more than conquerors." That means we win, leaving the enemy no hope for a comeback against us.

In fact, the only hope unbelievers have is to accept Jesus as their Savior and Lord, following our example. And our response to their persecution of us will speak the truth in love to them—if our response is to forgive them, to pray for them, and to witness to them of the wonderful love of God our Savior.

The magazine *The Voice of the Martyrs* shares many true stories of such forgiveness in the face of persecution and suffering. *Foxe's Book of Martyrs* by John Foxe documents true accounts through the ages of such forgiveness.

Self-Defense or Turn the Cheek?

Should we, therefore, not defend ourselves? Does "turn the other cheek" (see Matthew 5:39) mean that we must let people do violence to us and to our families? I cannot answer that for you. I believe that is something which each person must settle with the Lord. What I do know is that we are to forgive our enemies and to pray for them—even love them. But loving them does not mean calling their behavior right. Loving them means that we speak the truth in love to them. We tell them they need Jesus.

In the book of Esther, God records for us an example of fighting for survival against enemies set on the persecution and death of his people Israel. When the king could not reverse his ill-advised edict, he sent a proclamation throughout the land, granting

> the Jews in every city authority to unite to defend their lives. They were allowed to kill, slaughter, and annihilate anyone of any nationality or province who might attack them or their children and wives, and to take the property of their enemies. (Esther 8:11 NLT)

You can read the short Old Testament book of Esther for the background on this ruling.

Because circumstances vary, we have to be open to God's leading when severe persecution hits. We need to keep in mind that, "To every thing there is a season, and a time to every purpose under the heaven" (Ecclesiastes 3:1 KJV). And we need to be aware of what season we are in and what God's purpose is at the moment. How do we know these things? By prayer and the Word. The Holy Spirit will show us, even as Jesus promised.

Different situations will call for different responses. Our attitude should always be one of forgiveness and love, but the action we take will depend upon how the Lord leads in the moment, always within the guidelines of his Word.

In Matthew 5:39, he instructs his followers to "turn the other cheek." When he sent out the twelve and the seventy, he instructed them on what to carry, and it didn't include defensive weapons or even provision for the journey (Matthew 10:5–10; Mark 6:7–9; Luke 9:1–3; and Luke 10:1–4). Later, he instructed the disciples that if they had no sword, they should sell a garment and buy one (Luke 22:36).

This instruction resulted in Peter taking a sword to the garden of Gethsemane the night Jesus was betrayed. When Peter used the sword and cut off the servant's ear, Jesus healed the servant and told Peter that this wasn't the time for a sword. See Luke 22:49–51; Mark 14:47; and John 18:10–11. According to Matthew 26:53, Jesus could have called twelve legions of angels (between 120,000 and 188,000). But his response was to drink the cup which his Father had given him.

Persecution Disguised as Precautions

We have a cup to drink also. July 2020 will be remembered as a month of attack on Christians by leftist politicians, particularly in the state of California. And the attacks continued beyond that one month. The governor there, along with the governors in several other states, mandated that there could be NO SING-ING in church services. Then there were church closings, or allowing only fifty people in a church that could seat thousands. Mandatory mask orders followed. These were the manifestations of bullying by the cultural elite against Christians.

The rules were not officially legislated laws. They were mandates by individuals who hate Christ. They were "masked" as something beneficial—to limit the spread of Covid-19, but the same mandates did not apply to other gatherings. Casinos were allowed to open and run. Grocery chains and large department stores were allowed to operate with minimal regulation.

Many politicians who supported the restrictions on Christians contrarily supported the vocal, unmasked, and often violent protests in the streets. Cities were looted, burned, businesses destroyed, vehicles torched, and innocent people killed as the leftist protesters went unchecked. Meanwhile, several Christian pastors were arrested for holding church services, and parishioners were fined for attending "drive-in" services.

Many Christians recognized these actions as persecution—or, at the very least—bullying. But we have to accept it as God's will and respond however we are led by the Spirit to respond, whether to meekly obey and be silenced or sing out the praises of our God, lest the rocks cry out. Knowing God's will is essential to our decision.

What, in this country, has brought us to this crossroad, where to sing in church is "outlawed" by the command of a governor whose constitutional power is limited and not absolute? Was this oppression preceded by and a result of our temporary prosperity, which lulled us into a false sense of cultural security? The next chapter will consider this possibility.

And yet, the growing trend toward socialism brings with it a disdain for Christ and a contempt for Christians. The left talks about re-education camps for the children of Christians, and vaccinations to counteract a "gene" that makes us *dangerous, fanatical fundamentalists*. It would be laughable if not so pathetic. Christians are not the ones creating chaos in the USA. Christians are not the ones disrupting peace in the Mideast and Africa. Christians are the ones being persecuted, kidnapped, and killed. But to falsely accuse is a form of bullying. Its desired end is our silence and surrender.

Therefore, we need to speak the truth in love, hold forth the Word of Life, and shine as light in the darkness. We must prepare for persecution and always declare the way of salvation. Let us answer the bully with God's love.

And let us no longer be lulled by prosperity into a false sense of cultural security and programmed into silence.

Reflect Further

1. Read Acts 1:8; 4:13; 6:8–10; Matthew 7:6; Proverbs 26:4; and Titus 3:10. Whether we are actively being persecuted or simply being ignored, what is our responsibility to others?

2. What should be our motivation? What enables and empowers us?

3. Is there a time we should not share our testimony or speak the Word? When is that?

4. How do we know when to speak and when not to?

5. Read Matthew 16:1–3; 1 Thessalonians 5:1–6; Ephesians 5:8, 15–18; 1 Timothy 4:1–3; 2 Timothy 3:1–5; Jude 1:16–19; and 2 Peter 3:3–4. Describe the things from these verses that you see in our culture. With Matthew 24 in mind, would you say that we are in the "beginning of sorrows"? Do these conditions point toward a coming judgment?

6. What is the source of light that enables us to see clearly amidst the darkening culture? How can we be light for others, to warn them of what is coming and to lead them into peace and safety in Christ?

7. Reflect on times you have witnessed and people refused to hear. What about times when you witnessed and they did listen?

CHAPTER 8

Prosperity—Inverted Persecution

WE ENDED THE LAST CHAPTER talking about preparing for persecution and being on guard against prosperity. The persecution we face in the USA falls into other categories than the physical persecution in other places in the world. We face economic, social, political, and vocational persecution. We also face *inverted persecution*, which is my term for a focus on prosperity. Such focus leads to love of money, meaninglessness from excess, and success as the measure of one's worth.

We often think of prosperity as having to do with reaching goals, pushing forward, and achieving success. Mostly, though, it is closely associated with being financially successful. Prosperity is a product of materialism. So, how can it be persecution? Let's consider . . .

Two Stories of Success

Imagine a male CPA who specializes in trust accounting. Let's assume he has a few employees and an abundance of trusts for which he prepares monthly reports, handles their funds, and produces tax returns for them. He also does other tax returns as he builds his business.

Since tax accounting is seasonal, let's pretend he needs money to pay his receptionist, staff accountant, building lease, utilities, and other expenses, as well as his own salary. Let's assume income is low because he's in the off season. He has only the trust accounting fees this time of year, and they aren't enough. He's certain that in a few months, he'll have more income. But he needs money now. The bank won't advance him any funds. His wife has maxed his credit cards trying to impress the neighbors and her friends.

He thinks long and hard about this. Then he "borrows" from one of the trusts—just enough to get by. With the full intention of repaying it with interest, ASAP. And the next month—a different trust. Still with intent to repay. And then again the next month. He needs to start repaying those funds. But his only alternative is to sell personal assets, claim bankruptcy, or rob a bank. No. He's not considering that last one.

The amount adds up to an overwhelming total. And then he's discovered.

Or let's pretend it's a woman CPA, chief financial officer of a small manufacturing company publicly traded on NASDAQ. The company has reported slight losses for two years. One more loss year and their stock will be removed from the market. Her boss says, "Fix it. Hide the loss."

She can report truthfully and lose her job; she can resign and look for another job; or she can comply. She likes the power, prestige, and paycheck that comes with her title. So she sets out to "spin off" one product line into a separate company, assigning all the losses to it and preserving the rest of the company. In a year or so, they'll reacquire that product line. She knows this because they've done it previously—before her promotion from controller to CFO.

What can it hurt? The stock stays on the market, the company keeps going, and she still has a career. The long-term loss to stock owners is not even in her vision, nor is the possibility that the company may eventually declare bankruptcy.

We might be quick to condemn those accountants. We can see the harm in what they're doing. The dishonesty.

Now, let's pretend that both accountants attend church. They both believe that their lifestyles of luxury are the blessings of God on them. They think they are prospering as their souls prosper (3 John 1:2). They believe they are experiencing the abundant life which Jesus promised in John 10:10. Thus, the actions they take cannot be wrong.

Right?

This is why I use the term *inverted persecution*. It appears to be the opposite of persecution or suffering, but it comes as an attack against individuals and the church. Inspired by Satan, this attack originates from materialism and leads to idolatry. It is not merely the prosperity and security which many Christians enjoy as a result of hard work and doing life God's way. Rather it is the desire for and priority to acquire wealth and the material things it buys—the "love of money," which is the "root of all evil" (1 Timothy 6:10 KJV).

Love of Money

Many big-name speakers urge their congregations to expect wealth as a reward for their "right living" or their faith. These speakers proclaim prosperity as though it were the mark of godliness. Yet what does the Word say? "Yes, and all who desire to live a godly life in Christ Jesus will suffer persecution" (2 Timothy 3:12 MEV). So, persecution is a better gauge of godliness than prosperity is.

Furthermore, we are not to labor to lay up treasures on earth. Jesus said,

> "Don't store up treasures here on earth, where moths eat them and rust destroys them, and where thieves break in and steal. Store your treasures in heaven, where moths and rust cannot destroy, and thieves do not break in and steal. Wherever your treasure is, there the desires of your heart will also be." (Matthew 6:19–21 NLT)

What does a believer think who sits under prosperity preaching but never experiences wealth? How do people for whom prosperity remains elusive react to that message? How many sincere Christians have been made to feel worthless, unfavored, and betrayed? They suffer a unique persecution of the poor—at the hands of wealthy brothers and sisters in Christ. *Inverted persecution.*

How did we get here?

The United States has prospered materially far beyond the rest of the world since the end of WWII. While other nations may have pockets of affluence, their overall income level is generally less than that in the USA. Likewise, there are pockets of poverty in the USA, but the overall income level is generally greater than in the rest of the world.

Without quibbling over global GDP and GNI data, we all realize how wealthy our nation is, as a whole. One has only to travel to other countries to see how much we have here in comparison—even looking at small kitchen appliances and snack food choices. Add to that the level of affluence the media, entertainment, and sports worlds portray.

From the Sixties Forward

This disparity between the spending levels in the USA compared to the rest of the world was evident even in the mid to late 60s, as the middle class grew. It compounded the national unrest that arose over other important issues like civil rights and the Vietnam War.

Although the political protests of the 1960s were rooted in Marxist ideology, many who protested were so naïve as to not see that aspect of the movements. Some of us were really just wanting an end to discrimination, an end to the war so that the lives of the young men of our generation would be preserved, and an end to the love of money and things.

Ending the "love of money" would usher in, we thought, love of one another, which would result in racial equality, justice, and peace. (I suspect that many in Antifa and other groups who protest today are oblivious to the Marxist foundation of the protest's leaders, just as in the 1960s.)

Meaninglessness of Excess

Even though we might not have recognized it, our attitude about the acquisition of material wealth reflected the innate longing in our hearts for something eternal. We instinctively knew the principle of Matthew 6:24: "No one can serve two masters. For either he will hate the one and love the other, or else he will hold to the one, and despise the other. You cannot serve God and money" (MEV).

We longed for meaning, purpose, and truth. And we intuitively knew it was not to be found in stuff. Jesus affirms this knowledge in Luke 12:15: "Take heed and beware of covetousness. For a man's life does not consist in the abundance of his possessions" (MEV).

Moreover, part of the angst of the 1960s was a response to the perceived prosperity of the middle class. Teens, being impressionable, were encouraged by the enemy of our culture (Satan and those under his influence) to see all economic success as a product of greed and materialism. The same fallacy exists today. I just see more clearly now that the ones urging the response are themselves materialistic and greedy money-lovers. The ones they accuse of that are mostly hard-working individuals who enjoy the fruit of their labors.

Prosperity Message

However, there is a faction in the church that teaches we are not in God's will unless we are financially or materially prospering. Their emphasis for the "abundant life" is on the physical and economic realms, rather than the spiritual. Because John prayed for certain believers to "prosper and be in health" as their soul prospered (3 John 1:2 KJV), these erring teachers believe that financial prosperity and health are the correct gauges of spiritual well-being.

Furthermore, they interpret Jesus' promise that we would have life "more abundantly" (John 10:10 KJV) as meaning the acquisition of things. And those things go beyond necessities to the abundance of luxuries. Remember our two imaginary CPAs and how they justified wrongdoing to maintain prosperity.

The World's Measure of Success

We used to call this "keeping up with the Joneses." In the plastic society of the 1960s, everyone struggled for status symbols. If a neighbor bought a Chrysler, one needed a Cadillac. If a neighbor bought a Cadillac, one needed a BMW. If the neighbor bought a BMW, one needed a Mercedes. And so on. Bigger houses. Bigger yards. Backyard pools, decks, and equipment. A boat or yacht. Exotic vacations. Jewels, furs, artwork, furniture, Ivy League schools. And on and on. *Having* these things wasn't the real problem. The problem was *desiring* these things above all else and using their acquisition as a measure of success.

In reality, abundance clouds the cross, whereas intense need draws us to it. Prosperity is a bigger distraction from the Lord than is persecution, which tends to draw us closer to him.

And yet, in our culture, we strive for more stuff. We race to have the best in property or personal accomplishment. For many, material things have become an end in themselves— the motivation for life. Material things have replaced character traits like honesty, integrity, kindness to others, unity of purpose, patriotism, and helping the less fortunate. And the culture has darkened. The light of goodness, truth, and beauty has faded, being covered over with a lens of materialism.

Our responsibility and calling, as followers of Christ, is to walk in his light and to be light to others so they can see through this spirit of materialism that persists to this day. Exchanging our economic structure from capitalism to socialism is NOT the answer. The same greed exists under socialism. Giving up our God-given liberties for dependence upon the state is not the answer. The lust for things will still exist. It will just be that there are fewer people having a lot of stuff and more people having fewer things.

Socialism is Not the Answer

An example of a type of socialism occurred in the early church. It wasn't really socialism, though many today will argue that it was. Rather, it was a theocracy in which the members felt great unity with one another and a sense of immediacy regarding the Lord's return. Read Acts 4:32—5:12. Believers sold their land and houses and contributed the money to the church group. Everyone had property in common so that everyone's needs were met.

However, a certain couple, Ananias and Sapphira decided to profit from this arrangement by selling their land and donating part of it as if it were the whole amount. Their end game was to live off the church as long as possible and still have money left over when that arrangement ended. We infer this motive by the comments which Peter makes to them.

In Acts 5:4, Peter says, "While it remained unsold, was it not your own? And when it was sold, was it not under your authority? Why have you conceived this deed in your heart? You did not lie to men, but to God" (MEV). Peter makes it clear that Ananias had a right to both the land and the money received from its sale. His sin was in concocting a scheme to fool the believers and to lie to God about the proceeds and his commitment.

Both Ananias and his wife, Sapphira, paid for their sin with their lives. Too strict a punishment? No. Lying to God is a serious offense. We might wonder why they lied to God. Was it not to enable themselves to hang on to money? Thus, having that money was not wrong. Loving it was wrong, even in an economic structure where all things were held in common.

People who propose socialism today, as preferable to capitalism, make the argument based on identity politics rather than on a disdain of materialism. Those who propose it generally believe that they'll be the leaders who will have property that the workers forfeit. Of course, they don't tell the ordinary worker that. But materialism is still active in socialism as well as in capitalism.

Evidence of Materialism

How is the spirit of materialism evident today? Designer clothes, shoes, accessories. Knock-offs of designer products. Government corruption that allows lobbying—unrecorded payments to legislators to pass laws favoring the company that gives the most. Idolization of athletes and Hollywood stars who amass great wealth. Game shows like *The Price is Right*, *Let's Make a Deal*, *Wheel of Fortune*, and a host of other reruns and contest shows. Store catalogues and mailings, jokingly called "wish books." Black Friday sales as Christmas shopping sprees abound. The commercialization of Christmas. And on and on.

Does this mean that we should all sell our property and wear thrift store bargains and live on the streets? Of course not. It's not the having of things that brings darkness. It is the drive to acquire and hoard things that brings darkness. Not money, but the *love* of money. We dare not think that possessions will save us. We dare not gloat in having, as though our prosperity makes us someone special. We dare not insist that our wealth is self-generated, apart from God. We dare not trust in riches, because they can be consumed in a moment.

Jesus demonstrated this in a parable recorded in Luke 12:16–21 about a wealthy farmer who had a bumper crop so large his grain bins couldn't hold it all. His plan was to pull down his barns and build larger ones in which to store all his goods.

We might think that was a wise course of action. They probably didn't have common grain elevators where they could sell their grain and benefit up front. But here's the real sin of that man: "And I will say to my soul, Soul, you have many goods laid up for many years. Take rest. Eat, drink, and be merry" (v. 19 MEV). We cannot satisfy or save our soul with material possessions or wealth. We cannot depend upon our goods for our eternal—or even future—life.

God's answer to the man was this: "You fool! This night your soul will be required of you. Then whose will those things be which you have provided?" (v. 20 MEV). Jesus states his conclusion to the parable in verse 21: "So is he who stores up treasure for himself, and is not rich toward God" (MEV).

The man in the parable did not account for a tithe from his bumper crop. He did not even think to share with the poor. He didn't even plan to lay it in store and then plant again the next season and reap another good harvest. He was set for life, assured of the power and self-sufficiency of his possessions, rather than trusting in God. Unfortunately, many approach prosperity with this wrong attitude.

And it is the attitude that signals the sin. An attitude of self-sufficiency denies God's sovereignty. It marks rebellion against God's plan and provision.

Godly Prosperity

In contrast, when we praise God for what he supplies and give him the tithe, he is honored and pleased. That applies to our daily and future needs. We may have IRAs for retirement or savings for unplanned events like unemployment or disasters. But in all, we take it from his hand, keep things in perspective, and give God the glory.

Prosperity itself is not evil. God does bless some with financial success in this world. Having money and property doesn't make a person ungodly. How a person regards the wealth and what they do with it is what marks them as an obedient Christian or a materialistic rebel. Paul tells Timothy to withdraw from those who suppose "gain is godliness" (1 Timothy 6:5 KJV). In contrast, Paul says, "Yet true godliness with contentment is itself great wealth" (1 Timothy 6:6 NLT).

Paul considered this a topic worthy of more thought. He writes,

> After all, we brought nothing with us when we came into the world, and we can't take anything with us when we leave it. So if we have enough food and clothing, let us be content. But people who long to be rich fall into temptation and are trapped by many foolish and harmful desires that plunge them into ruin and destruction. For the love of money is the root of all kinds of evil. And some people, craving money, have wandered from the true faith and pierced themselves with many sorrows. (1 Timothy 6:7–10 NLT)

After exhortations to Timothy about right living, Paul concludes the discussion about wealth:

> Teach those who are rich in this world not to be proud and not to trust in their money, which is so unreliable. Their trust should be in God, who richly gives us all we need for our enjoyment. Tell them to use their money to do good. They should be rich in good works and generous to those in need, always being ready to share with others. By doing this they will be storing up their treasure as a good foundation for the future so that they may experience true life. (1 Timothy 6:17–19 NLT)

So it comes down to three questions:

1. Where is our focus?
2. In what or whom do we trust?
3. What do we do with what we have?

Jesus said, "But seek ye first the kingdom of God, and his righteousness; and all these things [clothing and food] shall be added unto you" (Matthew 6:33 KJV). *Where is our focus?* On God and his righteousness. *In whom do we trust?* In the heavenly Father himself, who will provide our needs.

What do we do with what we have? Receive it with thanksgiving, praise God for his provision, and share when we can. For that instruction, we look at Deuteronomy 15:11: "There will always be some in the land who are poor. That is why I am commanding you to share freely with the poor and with other Israelites in need" (NLT). That is the law behind the New Testament instructions of Paul to Timothy, quoted above.

Materialism Leads to Silence

What happens when the church sets aside the words spoken by Jesus and Paul regarding materialism?

In a culture that surrounds us with the drive for things, many have unconsciously fallen into the trap of materialism. Once there, we have become content and silent.

Even in churches where prosperity is not the focus, we have compromised to some extent. The abundance of things has become an idol. Testimonies are tarnished. The unbelieving world points a finger of judgment.

In this condition we have failed to speak against the spread of sin in our society. We have neglected to correct our children when they entered into unrighteousness. We have stopped being light, if we ever were. Our salt has lost its saltiness and has become unfit as a preservative or seasoning.

As a result, the enemy of the cross has gained more ground than when using direct persecution in times past and in other nations, where things are less plenteous. Hence, prosperity is a way to silence the Christian voice in a culture of increasing darkness. The unbelievers in the secular culture are influenced by the spirit of darkness—the devil, who works his evil in the culture through them.

Recognizing this is our key to correcting it.

How does this tie in to the larger subject at hand—how to speak truth to a culture that demands silence?

Demands of Silence

We have established that our culture does indeed demand silence from Christians. Especially since the 2020 coronavirus outbreak. Among other restrictions already discussed, we have been, in some cities and states, threatened with—or given—jail time for gathering to worship the Lord or for singing in church.

Before that, and continuing after, we have been told to not pray in public—like in a restaurant; not witness or hand out tracts, since the people we give them to often throw them on the ground, creating litter; not speak in school about God or even the possibility of a Creator/Intelligent Designer of the universe; not post on social media certain messages of truth; not mention the name of Jesus in an invocation at a public ceremony, such as a graduation; and so on. These forms of persecution are designed to silence us.

Persecution in Our Culture

In Chapter 3, you answered a question about what kinds of persecution we face in our culture today. One has only to research via duckduckgo.com or other Internet search engines to find examples of financial persecution by way of civil lawsuits, verbal harassment and silencing, and other disparaging accusations. Your answers might have included things like the following:

- lawsuits designed to destroy small businesses and bankrupt Christians
- unconstitutional "laws" making the free expression of our faith into something illegal
- court orders to remove emblems and symbols of our faith, including statues, the Ten Commandments, nativity sets, and even crosses in cemeteries
- attempts to regulate what topics ministers can and cannot preach about
- other censorship of the gospel message
- ridicule in school if we express faith in Christ and belief in creation
- in the political realm, scorn, media attacks, lies, false accusations, threatening, and mockery
- discrimination on the job by non-believers who sabotage the work of a believer
- edicts by governors that forbid Christians to sing in church services, while allowing singing in bars, clubs, protests, and other non-Christian gatherings
- Covid-19 rulings against holding church services, drive-in services, and evangelistic meetings, even outdoors

And the list could go on of things you've heard or read about from conservative news sources or have personally experienced. All these are activities of the enemy, Satan, who is insatiable. He inspires the enemies of the cross, darkens the culture with his evil thoughts, and ramps up persecution against God's people in this nation and in the world. Sometimes he uses secular leaders to carry out that persecution.

After the stoning of Stephen in the early church, believers were put to flight. They fled to other cities and areas, taking the gospel with them. Some were arrested and taken to prison, as we see in Acts 8:1–3. Imagine the anguish and trouble of families being ripped apart as parents were taken to prison, leaving children alone. This happens today in other countries. In many nations, Christians are chased out of their homes, forced off their property, and killed for their faith in Christ.

Thus, on one hand Christians suffer persecution, and on the other, they wallow in affluence and hide their light lest they lose their abundance. We in the United States have little understanding of the experience of persecuted Christians in other lands.

But we will learn. The beginning of hostile persecution in the USA—starting with imposed silence—signals a change coming. Christians here are being forced to wake up and make a stand. We must choose. Continue to hide in silence or speak out for Christ? Continue in luxury or suffer loss for Christ?

Pastors and churchgoers who have bought into the prosperity message tarnish the message of truth. They dim the light of the testimony of yielded believers by making the acquisition of wealth the goal of "spiritual" life. And that is not our goal.

True Spiritual Prosperity

Instead of seeking things, we are to seek Christ and his righteousness first, above all else, and trust him to supply all our physical needs, by way of job, income source, or divine provision. We share with those in need. We shine light into the world to light the way for others. Our life speaks truth to the very culture that tells us to be silent.

That's why the culture, which has chosen darkness, wants us to be caught up in its quest for *things*. If it can get our eyes off Christ and onto material possessions (even simply our needs), then it dims the light that would otherwise shine in our lives.

However, we're not up against just an inanimate culture. The culture is comprised of people whose minds are darkened by and influenced by the devil. We see this in 2 Corinthians 4:3–4, where Paul writes,

> If the Good News we preach is hidden behind a veil, it is hidden only from people who are perishing. Satan, who is the god of this world, has blinded the minds of those who don't believe. They are unable to see the glorious light of the Good News. They don't understand this message about the glory of Christ, who is the exact likeness of God. (NLT)

Ephesians 6:12 lets us know the scope of the satanic enemy's influence in our culture.

Thus, we must acknowledge that the unbelieving culture is inspired, motivated, and directed by the enemy, Satan. Our calling is to shine into that dark culture, enlightening the eyes of those whose hearts are open. We are to show by our lives the truth, goodness, and beauty of Christ. We are to speak with love the truth of the gospel. And we are to live that truth daily as proof of its reality.

Our attitudes toward possessions should line up with our claim to "seek first the kingdom of God and His righteousness" (Matthew 6:33 MEV). If we are caught up in materialism, our words ring false, our voice sounds flat, and our light wanes dim. Therefore, we must speak truth with the Word of God, the word of our testimony, and with our very lives—without focus on material prosperity.

Reflect Further

1. Read Luke 6:38; Acts 20:35; Ephesians 4:28; 1 Thessalonians 4:11–12; and 2 Thessalonians 3:10–12. If God has promised to supply all needs, why must we work, as Paul says, in order to eat?

2. What about people who can't work? Is it our responsibility to support them, especially those in our household, family, and church? Read Galatians 2:10.

3. In this nation of abundance, if everyone who could do so would take care of a homeless person or family, would homelessness disappear? Is that practical?

4. In Mark 14:7, Jesus says that we have the poor with us always. What does he mean by that statement? Is it wrong to want to end poverty?

5. Read Proverbs 23:4; Matthew 6:19–21, 25–33; and Philippians 4:19. What are some of the means by which God meets our physical needs? How many of them involve our participation?

6. Paul says in 2 Corinthians 4:18, "For the things which are seen are temporal; but the things which are not seen are eternal" (KJV). Does that help explain why we are told not to lay up treasures on earth? Does the parable about the man building a bigger barn (Luke 12:16–21) reinforce this?

7. Read Ephesians 1:7; 3:8, 16. What kind of wealth and treasure does Jesus have? Can we claim it too?

8. Read Matthew 7:7–11. Jesus says our heavenly Father will give us "good things" if we ask him. What must be our attitude in order to receive these gifts?

Should We Expect to be Persecuted?

IN THE MIDST OF the prosperity in our nation, biblical persecution seems out of place. Yet it is real. Throughout the world, Christians are persecuted. And we have seen that the trend in this nation is toward persecution.

We saw in opening chapters that the early church faced continual persecution that worsened over time. The believers refused to remain silent in the face of this persecution. But they didn't clamor and complain about the persecution. They didn't join together and lobby the Pharisees and Sadducees to convince them to stop persecuting them. They didn't file petitions with Rome, seeking an end to the religious persecution.

In fact, the only one to appeal to Rome was Paul, who did it to gain an entrance into the palace to minister the gospel to Caesar and those of his household. Paul wrote great words of encouragement to Timothy and urged him to

> never be ashamed to tell others about our Lord. And don't be ashamed of me, either, even though I'm in prison for him.

> With the strength God gives you, be ready to suffer with me
> for the sake of the Good News. (2 Timothy 1:8 NLT)

In short, he urged Timothy to partake of the persecution for the gospel, and to do it as a natural outworking of the miraculous power of God.

Lest we think that Paul only gave that instruction to Timothy because Timothy was following him in the ministry, let's look at what Paul tells the *pew sitters* of Philippi: "For you have been given not only the privilege of trusting in Christ but also the privilege of suffering for him" (Philippians 1:29 NLT). We all have the privilege of suffering for Christ.

Indeed, one of the proofs of the reality of the gospel is that serious believers are willing to suffer persecution for the truth of Jesus Christ. Is there another worldview that offers persecution to its followers? Christianity holds forth the promise of eternal blessing to a greater degree for those who suffer in this life.

Other worldviews may offer wealth and fame in this life, but nothing for eternity. Most of them deny the reality of eternity or offer the fleeting pleasures of this life as the reward in the next—as though the eternal soul could be satisfied with sexual activity. How demeaning to the concept of an eternal spirit!

The Bible says much more about suffering and persecution than it does prosperity and material wealth. Paul talked of suffering "the loss of all things" to "win Christ" (Philippians 3:8 KJV). He desired to "know him, and the power of his resurrection, and the fellowship of his sufferings, being made conformable unto his death" (Philippians 3:10 KJV).

Fellowship of Suffering

Knowing the fellowship of Jesus' sufferings means to suffer persecution, even unto death if necessary, right along with him. We cannot expect to know the power of God unless we're willing to experience the suffering of Christ. Philippians 3:10 emphasizes this: "I want to know Christ and experience the mighty power that raised him from the dead. I want to suffer with him, sharing in his death" (NLT).

The goal to which Paul pressed (Philippians 3:11, 14) was to be a fully dedicated follower of Christ, destined to "receive the heavenly prize" (v. 14 NLT). It is that place in heaven that the bride of Christ will occupy, as a company of spiritually mature believers who have dedicated their lives to Christ even under persecution. This is what Paul means in vv. 8–9, when he writes, "so that I could gain Christ and become one with him" (NLT).

Romans 8:17 makes this point: "And if children, then heirs; heirs of God, and joint-heirs with Christ; if so be that we suffer with him, that we may be also glorified together" (KJV). A joint-heir is a spouse and inherits more by default than offspring or siblings. All who are born-again are children of God, and therefore heirs. Not all believers yield fully to the Lord and to the Holy Spirit. Those who do are destined to become joint-heirs.

Paul emphasizes this point to Timothy in 2 Timothy 2:12 when he says, "If we suffer, we shall also reign with him: if we deny him [by refusing to suffer persecution], he will also deny us [the privilege of reigning with him]" (KJV). I have supplied in the brackets the words needed to make the verse clear. That sentiment is emphasized in a note in the New King James Version, and it aligns with verse 13, which declares, "If we are faithless, He remains faithful; He cannot deny Himself" (NKJV). This seems contradictory, but let's look at it from a modern perspective.

For example, if we own a business that we want to leave to our grown son or daughter, but they refuse to learn the trade and appear disinterested in it, we probably will find another option. We won't disown them—they will always be our child. But we won't reward them with a ready-made business. They haven't, in a sense, "suffered for it." They haven't worked that business alongside of us, thereby learning how to run it.

Thus, in 2 Timothy 2, Paul is saying that Christ's spirit indwells us when we are born again, making us one with him. He cannot deny that we belong to him, but he can deny us the privilege of ruling with him if we decline to suffer with him.

Jesus taught this truth in the parable of the talents (Luke 19:11–27). Verse 27 makes it clear that the unbeliever gets death, while the un-yielded believer gets simply no reward. Believers who waste their opportunities and refuse to suffer with Christ will still be in heaven, but they will forfeit rewards.

First Century Christians Expected Persecution

In the early church, believers expected to be persecuted for Christ and willingly suffered for the gospel according to God's power. Paul told Timothy, "Yes, and all who desire to live a godly life in Christ Jesus will suffer persecution" (2 Timothy 3:12 MEV). This is still true today, especially in other countries. Is it surprising, then, that the trend of our culture is increasingly in this direction? Are we prepared for it?

Can we answer as Paul did in 2 Timothy 1:12?

> That is why I am suffering here in prison. But I am not ashamed of it, for I know the one in whom I trust, and I am

sure that he is able to guard what I have entrusted to him until the day of his return. (NLT)

Can we follow the admonition in verse 13: "Hold on to the pattern of wholesome teaching you learned from me—a pattern shaped by the faith and love that you have in Christ Jesus" (NLT)? Will we obey verse 14: "Through the power of the Holy Spirit who lives within us, carefully guard the precious truth that has been entrusted to you" (NLT)?

These are questions we each must be prepared to answer and act upon.

Mitigating the Suffering

Is there something we can do to delay the persecution, or at least to lessen it? Paul mentioned his Roman citizenship to be allowed a chance to speak to the people (Acts 21:39). He mentioned it again to avoid an immediate flogging without trial (Acts 22:25). Yet in 2 Corinthians 11:23–28, he lists the times he was beaten, imprisoned, in shipwrecks, and facing other dangers. His Roman citizenship did not protect him from those things. He allowed himself to become a prisoner of Rome so he could witness to Caesar and Caesar's household.

This is not to say that believers should vote for a godless candidate—one who supports infanticide, taxpayer-funded abortion on demand, and sexual perversion and gender confusion—just so they can suffer for Christ. Being in this free nation, we need to stand for God's righteousness, speak the truth in love, and live as good examples of his holiness. We need to vote according to our conscience. Can we conscientiously vote for someone who supports the torture and killing of pre-born babies? Since no human candidate is sinless, where do we draw the line? Each individual must pray through that and be led of the Holy Spirit.

This much I know: God has blessed us to be born into a nation where our liberty is guaranteed by the constitution and where we have a right to vote for our leaders. Thus, we insult God if we fail to hold dear that liberty by refusing to vote. Though we are citizens of heaven, and though the kingdom of God is that which we seek, we do have a civic responsibility to attempt to preserve the union.

It's a lot like the parable of the talents. The servant who buried his talent lost all rewards. Claiming to be too spiritual to vote is hypocrisy. So is claiming to be too spiritually mature to be cumbered with guiding others into paths of righteousness. We are called to be salt and light, not unmined rock salt in a dark cavern.

Yes, we who have studied prophecy know the ending. We are primarily concerned with that and with our Lord, as he brings us to that end. However, we know we must, like the parable says, "Do business till I come" (Luke 19:13 NKJV). We should be, as Paul says, "redeeming the time, because the days are evil" (Ephesians 5:16 NKJV).

Our Responsibility to Our Culture

So what is our responsibility in and for our culture? Our role in the politics of our nation? Besides shining as light and speaking the truth in love (as already discussed in earlier chapters), there are some specific things we can and should do.

First, we are to pray for elected officials and those whom they lawfully appoint (1 Timothy 2:1–2). The purpose is so that we "may lead a quiet and peaceful life in all godliness and honesty" (MEV). What about elected officials and appointees who stand against biblical morality and issue edicts that promote ungodliness, chaos, and harm to others? All the more reason to pray for them, that they would come to the Lord, repent, and change their policies.

Second, when given an opportunity, we should witness to them, as Paul did, reaching many in Caesar's household (Philippians 4:22). Most of us won't have the kind of opportunities that Paul had. But we don't know what lies ahead for us. So we need to be sure we are ready to testify of the saving grace of Jesus Christ and the new creation life of godliness.

In our nation, God has blessed us with the privilege and responsibility to vote. That is the third thing we can do to influence the culture. In voting, we can voice our opinion as to whom we want to have the authority over us, politically. We ought to vote according to God's righteousness. This doesn't mean to demand a sinless candidate (for "all have sinned"—Romans 3:23 KJV).

It means to examine the platform and promises of the candidates. It means to NOT vote for those who stand for the murder of pre-born babies, for the spread of falsehoods in grades K-12, or for the validation of perverse lifestyles such as homosexuality and pedophilia. We need to be informed by the candidates themselves, not by the portrayal of them in a biased media. We need to vote responsibly, in accord with the Word and righteousness of God.

Fourth, we must take a stand on issues in the culture, without compromise. Paul says in Romans 12:9, "Don't just pretend to love others. Really love them. Hate what is wrong. Hold tightly to what is good" (NLT). And his Word tells us what is good. He expands on this in Ephesians 5:6–12:

> Don't be fooled by those who try to excuse these sins, for the anger of God will fall on all who disobey him. Don't

participate in the things these people do. For once you were full of darkness, but now you have light from the Lord. So live as people of light! For this light within you produces only what is good and right and true. Carefully determine what pleases the Lord. Take no part in the worthless deeds of evil and darkness; instead, expose them. It is shameful even to talk about the things that ungodly people do in secret. (NLT)

The fifth thing is an attitude we need to have in all the other actions. We need to keep things in perspective, viewing all things in the *light of eternity*. In 2 Corinthians 4:17–18, Paul says,

For our present troubles are small and won't last very long. Yet they produce for us a glory that vastly outweighs them and will last forever! So we don't look at the troubles we can see now; rather, we fix our gaze on things that cannot be seen. For the things we see now will soon be gone, but the things we cannot see will last forever. (NLT)

Thus, the political state of our nation is only temporal. Even if our liberties vanish and we are given over to socialism (communism) or fall into the chaos of sin and lawlessness—it would only be temporal. We need to keep that in mind. The eternal is what counts.

Finally, if God calls us to a political office as our vocation, we ought to fulfill it according to his will. Paul assures us that Jesus will help us in whatever our calling is. He says in Hebrews 13:21, that our Lord will "equip you in every good thing to do His will, working in us that which is pleasing in His sight, through Jesus Christ, to whom be the glory forever and ever. Amen" (NASB).

Thus, working in whatever vocation we have, we can be sure the Lord will help us. And as we do the work honestly and heartily, he will get the glory. Paul mentions the importance of working in 1 Thessalonians 4:11 and Titus 3:14. These don't specify politics, but it can be considered "good deeds to meet pressing needs" (Titus 3:14 NASB). What is more pressing than having honest politicians and appointees with integrity and godliness?

Old Testament Examples

There are several examples in the Old Testament of God's people being used to fulfill roles in the government of nations. Esther was brought to the kingdom of a Gentile ruler for "such a time as this" (Esther 4:14 MEV). Through her, the people of Israel were spared from certain annihilation. If you are unfamiliar with her story, read the short book of Esther and see how God ordained her involvement in the government of a foreign power.

Daniel and the three who were delivered from the fiery furnace are examples of God setting his people in places of authority in governments of non-Israelites. Read the short book of Daniel.

Joseph, second to Pharaoh, ruled over Egypt, an otherwise ungodly nation. We've seen his story in earlier chapters.

Moses was raised as the son of Pharaoh's daughter. In his case, God did not choose to deliver Israel by a national decree of Moses. He had Moses flee the rulership of Egypt and return under God's authority and miracle-working power to lead his people out of Egypt. We read of Moses in Hebrews 11:24–26:

> By faith Moses, when he became of age, refused to be called the son of Pharaoh's daughter, choosing rather to suffer affliction with the people of God than to enjoy the pleasures of sin for a time. He esteemed the reproach of Christ as greater riches than the treasures in Egypt, for he looked to the reward. (MEV)

Even Lot, who was "sick of the shameful immorality of the wicked people around him" (2 Peter 2:7 NLT), "sat in the gate of Sodom" (Genesis 19:1 KJV) as one of the men governing the city. Though he did nothing to limit the sinfulness of the rest of the city, he did keep himself, and the angels who visited, free from homosexuality. And God delivered him from the city.

During the kingdom years of Israel, even when the kingdom was split, God sent prophets to speak to the kings, both the good ones and the evil ones. Those prophets had their place in the governing of the nations, though often they were ignored and persecuted.

In Our Day

If God gives us a place and job in the political realm, we must fulfill it. If he sends us simply to speak to those in authority, we must speak his truth. But we cannot deny that he has given every believer the task of "shining like bright lights in a world full of crooked and perverse people" (Philippians 2:15 NLT). In that role, we are to "hold forth the word of life" (v. 16 MEV). The Holy Spirit empowers us to fulfill this charge, as we yield to him and walk in the Spirit.

When we fail to speak, we abandon the culture. When we take our faith into the privacy of four walls and a roof, the culture abandons us—and the principles and moral guidelines of the Judeo-Christian heritage.

This has happened, and the nation has veered off course. We can't place the sole blame upon the LGBTQ movement, the abortion clinics and pro-abortionists, the God-rejecting political leaders of the left, or Hollywood with its portrayal of sin as the ultimate satisfaction. We must accept our own share of blame and guilt for hiding our light under a basket and refusing to proclaim the truth of God's Word. The results of our privatization are now being felt through persecution which will worsen over time.

Persecution is Expected

As we have seen, though, such persecution is to be expected. The night he was betrayed, Jesus told the disciples, "In the world you will have tribulation. But be of good cheer. I have overcome the world" (John 16:33 MEV). The Greek word translated "tribulation" means "pressure" and is also translated affliction, anguish, burdened, persecution, and trouble. We are to expect trouble—and even persecution—in this life. We are also to expect victory through Jesus.

Peter writes about "manifold temptations" (1 Peter 1:6 KJV), where "temptations" means "adversity" or "putting to proof," and "the trial of your faith" (v. 7 KJV), where "trial" means "testing." Thus, adversity and persecution are sent to test and to prove our faith.

However, it is not just any pressure or adversity. If the trouble comes as a consequence of our wrong behavior, we can't claim to be suffering with Christ or to be in a trial of faith. We're simply facing the consequences of our actions.

Peter makes this clear in 1 Peter 4:12–16:

> Dear friends, don't be surprised at the fiery trials you are going through, as if something strange were happening to you. Instead, be very glad—for these trials make you partners with Christ in his suffering, so that you will have the wonderful joy of seeing his glory when it is revealed to all the world.
>
> If you are insulted because you bear the name of Christ, you will be blessed, for the glorious Spirit of God rests upon you. If you suffer, however, it must not be for murder, stealing, making trouble, or prying into other people's affairs. But it is no shame to suffer for being a Christian.

> Praise God for the privilege of being called by his name! (NLT)

Indeed, we are in good company when we are persecuted for being Christians. In fact, Jesus says we're blessed:

> Blessed are you when people insult you and persecute you, and falsely say all kinds of evil against you because of Me. Rejoice and be glad, for your reward in heaven is great; for in this same way they persecuted the prophets who were before you. (Matthew 5:11–12 NASB)

We are blessed to be persecuted. We are in good company with the prophets, the early disciples, and Christians today in other lands.

Global Persecution

An article on the Open Doors organization website says that "today, *more than 340 million people worldwide* face persecution and discrimination for their faith. That's 1 in 8 Christians who are targeted, discriminated against and attacked for following Jesus."[1] Since few in the United States are actively persecuted, to reach that ratio globally, the number abroad must be more than 1 in 8.

That article, which lists ten dangerous places to live in the world, asserts that "Behind every statistic and fact is a life, a family, a church that represents deep suffering but also courage and resilient faith. People who know the consequences yet still choose Jesus."[2] O that we could claim the same faithful resolve in this country!

As we think about the present national turmoil, we can see some things that spring from current events but that are not necessarily direct persecution. These things might be an overt assault on Christianity, and some people believe they are. They also might be simply used that way by the devil, though the humans "in charge" don't realize it. Hopefully, by the time this book is published, the whole Covid-19 affair will be behind us.

National Chaos

However, many of us will remember 2020-2021 when schools and the economy were shut down, churches closed, and many liberties foregone. Many lost loved ones to the virus. Much social tumult arose over the issues of wearing masks, treatment of the virus in early stages, social distancing, and churches remaining closed while bars and casinos were allowed to open. Families were forbidden to visit their loved ones in nursing homes, and many nursing home residents faced loneliness and isolation.

Add to that the destruction of statues and historical sites. And the riots in many major cities where anti-Americans burned, looted, destroyed property, and killed innocent bystanders. Compound that with the order by democrat mayors for the police to stand down and let the rioters burn and loot. And then add the call for the defunding of police departments and canceling icons like Aunt Jemima syrup, Uncle Ben's rice, Mr. Potato Head, and several books by Dr. Seuss. It's difficult not to see this as the "perilous times" of which Paul warns us in 2 Timothy 3:1 KJV.

In the midst of this disorder, we are called to show love to others (Ephesians 5:2), to offer comfort through the Word (2 Corinthians 1:4), to remain joyous and confident in Christ (Philippians 4:4), and to not be afraid (Joshua 1:9). The Covid-19 scare will pass. But other crises will follow. Chaos, confusion, and unrest are signs of the time. Our response testifies of our faith and can speak peace in the midst of that turbulence.

However, politically it seems we are in for increased persecution. After one day in a new administration more leftist than many people expected, we see the advancement of confusion and sin. We find our nation once again funding global abortions as well as our own, once again confusing genders in sports and bathroom use, and more than ever silencing the voices of Christians and others who see the folly in the advancing socialism.

This trend is nothing new. Our nation was set on this trajectory decades ago. Jack Lee writes in a blog on Patheos,

> If we are honest with ourselves, we lost our country 50 or so years ago when the church rolled over and allowed liberalism to plant itself within our higher education systems. After that, it was only a matter of time. Such concessions have changed the moral standard of what is culturally permissible and opened biblical Christianity in America to persecution.[3]

The eventual end of this trend will be open persecution of Christians, because the worldly church compromised and conceded, remaining silent when it should have spoken out. In his blog, Lee encourages American Christians to prepare for this persecution. He writes,

> American Christians, who desire to live godly, conservative, biblically-oriented lives, need to prepare themselves and their families for suffering. The writing has been on the wall for some time, decades even, yet the church has done little to stop it. Instead, like a row of dominoes, she has fallen over on issue after issue. The church has watched while influential institutions and religious leaders denied the miracles of Jesus, rejected the inerrancy of scripture, allowed for abortifacient birth control methods, legalized abortion, endorsed gay marriage, and even embraced critical race theory.[4]

But in reality, it had to be this way. Biblically, we should expect persecution. Jesus said it would come. It came to the early church and to believers throughout the following centuries in other parts of the world. In fact, as to our place in the world, Lee says,

> We were never promised safety in Christ. The opposite is true; we are promised persecution (2 Timothy 3:12). A time is approaching when going to church will be dangerous (and I do not mean because of a virus). Now is the time to prepare and reinforce healthy habits. Instill in your children the need and benefit of attending church weekly. Go and be fed the gospel.[5]

We are on the verge of a change in America. Even if conservatives regain the houses of congress in 2022, the die is cast. Without a national repentance for the sins of abortion, homosexuality, other sexual sins, and the rejection of Christ, the USA will face God's judgment. Lee states,

> The world is changing, and it is time we solidify in our minds who we are in Christ, commit ourselves to corporate worship, sound philosophies, and Christian worldviews. Persecution is coming; this seems inevitable. Yet, we are not without hope. On the contrary, we have enough hope to fill a new generation of believers.[6]

Indeed, all is not grim. We have God's promise to be with us through persecution and to reward us for our suffering. After all, Jesus Christ suffered for us, giving us the example of how to suffer. Peter writes, "For God called you to do good, even if it means suffering, just as Christ suffered for you. He is your example, and you must follow in his steps" (1 Peter 2:21 NLT).

Reflect Further

1. Many Scriptures give God's promise to be with us. Read Romans 8:35–39; Hebrews 13:5–6; Matthew 28:20; Deuteronomy 31:7–8; and Joshua 1:5, 9. Think of the slaughter

of God's people (Romans 8:36) in light of God's presence with them and his ability to protect them. How can we be "more than conquerors" if we are killed?

2. What other verses can you find that promise God's presence with us?

3. How should we feel about knowing that God is always with us?

4. Was God faithful to be with Moses and then with Joshua in Israel's history? Does he continue to be faithful today to the church as well as to Israel?

5. Read Daniel 2:20–22; 4:17, 24–26, 32–35; Psalm 75:7; Jeremiah 18:7–10; Psalm 33:12; 144:15; and Proverbs 29:2. If God controls who rules over nations, as these verses suggest, why should we bother to vote? Do these Scriptures apply to monarchies only? Does God use our votes to set up whom he will? What if people rig the elections, as in some socialist countries?

6. Consider 2 Chronicles 7:14. If our nation is headed the wrong way, can prayer reverse that slide into sin? Can our prayers change the course of the nation?

7. Does our nation have Judeo-Christian roots? Can we expect God's continued blessing if our politicians and culture deny those roots and insist that the will of God has no place in Congress?

8. While we pray for our nation to repent, turn around, and be revived, should we prepare for persecution?

9. Does the prospect of persecution alarm you? What verses should help you face your fear?

CHAPTER 10

Real Love as Voice

IN THE LATE 1960S, my friends of color and I wanted an end to the "us and them" mentality. "We all bleed red" was our slogan. We joined together in what we called *the Zebra Club*—black and white together.

In those days, the term "colored" was rejected by the college age blacks I knew, who preferred the term "black." One friend told me that the term "colored," always made him think of a box of crayons. We laughed about the different shades of skin. Whites are not true white. We are pink, tan, orange, eggshell, and other various shades of off-white. And, of course, blacks are not true black, but various shades of brown. I've known whites who tanned in the summer to a darker shade of brown than some of my black friends. It's ridiculous to clash over skin color.

And yet our nation is still locked in racial conflict. In the late 60s, I felt hope for a change. And so did my friends.

However, the assassination of Dr. Martin Luther King, Jr., shattered that hope, and with it, unity. Those whom I had marched shoulder to shoulder with suddenly viewed me as an outsider because of my whiteness, though I claimed to be "not white, but polka dot," having freckles.

After the 60s, it seems that opportunities for blacks increased. Interracial marriage became accepted, and many people of color earned status in the professions, in their own businesses, in management positions, and in blue-collar vocations. Many white Christians, pleased with the progress, turned their attention elsewhere.

Trouble Ahead

As the moral fabric of the nation broke down and, with it, the traditional family structure, the inner cities deteriorated. Drugs permeated those areas, and gangs became the norm.

It's like there were two groups of people of color: those who exited the inner cities, took advantage of the opportunities, and achieved success; and those who were trapped in the inner cities with no motivation to escape but with an innate desire for a better life and for respect. These groups are not exclusive to people of color. Some whites achieve success, while others are stuck in the same scenario of poverty and crime.

Somehow, we need to help these economically challenged groups to step into the realm of success that the first group has attained. The group that contains my current friends of color, who are my brothers and sisters in Christ.

Though the assassination of Dr. King put out the light of hope for many people, it is our responsibility, as followers of Christ, to be light in this culture. We are to be the light that Dr. King was, to work and love our way toward the realization of his dream, which ought to be our dream too. This is possible only in Christ, the True Light. His love alone can end racism.

Another factor in the continued racial disparity is the media emphasis upon the incidents of police brutality that are admittedly very wrong but sometimes the fault of a perpetrator who resists arrest. The police will enforce their authority over a person resisting or endangering them, black or white. Sometimes with excessive force.

However, there is much to be said for the occurrence in some cities of the harassment of innocent people of color. We've all seen it in television shows and movies. Many have experienced it. All the more reason to instruct our youth—of all races and ethnicities—to be respectful toward police, to follow instructions, and to present no threats.

Optimally, if those living in inner cities were to become born-again, their entire lives would change, and these issues would go away. They would have joy, motivation, purpose, and meaning. Only the love of Christ can accomplish that— love working in and through us to share Christ with them.

Small Acts of Prejudice

I remember having a black college student tell me that he was tired of being treated suspiciously every time he entered a shop. I didn't have a clue as to what he meant until several years later when I experienced it myself.

I entered a well-known pharmacy to purchase heads for my electric toothbrush. I had been fighting asthmatic bronchitis, so I hadn't felt much like fixing up. I was in baggy sweat pants, a hoodie, and well-worn sneakers. My hair was a disaster with an inch of gray roots showing, and I had skipped the make up. In those days, I carried a backpack instead of a purse.

The store manager met me just inside the door and asked if he could help me. He led me back to the toothbrush aisle, stood while I selected a package, and escorted me to the cash register. I had planned to pick up chips or snacks of some kind, but he didn't seem to want me to browse. I kept wondering why I was getting this special treatment. After deciding which credit card to use, I paid and left.

It wasn't till I was outside that I realized why I received such unusual treatment. He thought I was a homeless person and was planning to shoplift!

In that moment, I remembered what my student had told me several years prior. And I knew what he meant. It didn't matter that he was honest, hardworking, clean-cut, and educated. Some people suspected the worst of him because of his skin color.

That is the problem we need to eradicate. And only love can do that. The love of and for Jesus Christ.

Christ is the Answer

Many people today blame the church for the continued tension. We need to stop blaming, stop playing the victim, stop accusing, and stop stereotyping, and begin seeing one another as Christ sees us, as one in him (Galatians 3:28). We need to see as valuable to God those who are not yet "in him," because he desires that all would be saved and "come to the knowledge of the truth" (1 Timothy 2:4 NKJV).

When people try to engage us in blame-throwing, name-calling, victimizing, or playing the victim, we need to refuse that negative dialogue and shine as light, speaking the truth in love—the truth that Jesus loves all, died for all, and deeply desires all to be saved.

People who reject this conversation will not profit from, learn about, or be appeased by any other conversation or concession given. We can't insult them into the kingdom. We can't compromise them into the kingdom. But we can invite them into the kingdom of God. And we can pray.

When Jesus sent out seventy disciples to prepare the way for him, he instructed them, "The harvest is great, but the workers are few. So pray to the Lord who is in charge of the harvest; ask him to send more workers into his fields" (Luke 10:2 NLT). The analogy is that people who are ready to receive Christ are "the harvest" and people ministering the Word to them are "the workers." So, whether we work or pray for workers, we are helping in the harvest of souls.

Complications in the Culture

However, the culture has taken a turn away from Christ and away from improved race relations. It rebukes all who cling to the perspective of the mid-twentieth century—that blacks and whites can work together. That we can continue to make great strides toward equal opportunity, fair treatment, and respect for and prosperity of all Americans willing to work. We are, after all, only one race—human.

Are there still areas of injustice or inequality of outcome? Yes. Are those solely because of white racism? No. Some are. And, yes, there are places where blacks are targeted and mistreated and where people are racist. There are also places where whites are mistreated and targeted and where people are racist. I have a white friend whose experience with police was terrifying. But that was only one officer out of thousands. Weeding out the bad ones is preferable to defunding them all.

I can't list all the successful black business owners, doctors, lawyers, accountants, athletes, pastors, writers, actors, musicians, educators, entertainers, speakers, blue-collar workers, and politicians. There are too many to list. There are enough to prove that this nation has moved beyond slavery, segregation, racism, and discrimination.

In spite of that progress, a past president and his wife campaigned on "fundamentally changing" this nation and "changing its history." Though the work toward that end halted for four years, it appears to be swiftly moving again.

Two false ideas set on making these fundamental changes have swept through the culture. Because these errors oppose Christianity and our Christian heritage, we need to fight them with prayer, knowledge, and the Word of truth spoken in love. They are critical race theory and the 1619 project. You may have heard a lot about these ideas and programs. Let's consider them separately.

Critical Race Theory

A recent development in race relations is the emergence of critical race theory. The idea has a vague, postmodern name that communicates nothing. Most Americans don't have a clue as to what it says or represents. And that's how the left wants it. If parents and citizens don't understand what is being taught in public schools, they can't complain or counter it. That's why it is "critical" that we know all about it and can counter its detrimental effect.

Tremendously helpful to me was the March 2021 issue of *Imprimis*, a publication of Hillsdale College. Christopher F. Rufo presents an article, "Critical Race Theory: What It Is and How to Fight It." The article is available online at https://imprimis.hillsdale.edu/critical-race-theory-fight/.

In the article, Rufo traces the theory's Marxist roots and shows evidence of its intent to destroy capitalism, end property ownership rights, and redistribute land and wealth to non-white races.[1] The theory replaces equality with equity, individual rights with group rights, individual identity with group stereotyping, and, consequently, content of character with color of skin. Rufo says that, "critical race theory prescribes a revolutionary program that would overturn the principles of the Declaration and destroy the remaining structure of the Constitution."[2]

Many readers may recognize the theory from required training sessions at their place of employment. These workshops have occurred from warehouses to government agencies, from professional offices to manufacturing sites. White workers are told that all whites are racist and must apologize for their white privilege. Any attempt to contradict that narrative is met with scorn and shaming. The extent to which this "re-education" occurs is shocking, although those who have sat in on the workshops understand.

Furthermore, the theory has been woven into the educational system even at the first grade level. In his article in *Imprimis*, Rufo, an investigative journalist, exposes several cases of this intimidation of white students and teachers. He has a database that exceeds 1,000 true stories and cautions that the "ideology will not stop until it has devoured all of our institutions."[3]

Think about it for a moment. Judging a whole group of people based on the color of their skin has always characterized racism. Yet critical race theory judges all white people as racist on the basis of their white skin, not their actions or actual beliefs. Thus, critical race theory is racism against whites.

And we cannot defeat racism with racism. Dr. Martin Luther King, Jr. makes this point beautifully in his well-known and often-quoted statement:

> Returning hate for hate multiplies hate, adding deeper darkness to a night already devoid of stars. Darkness cannot drive out darkness; only light can do that. Hate cannot drive out hate; only love can do that.[4]

Only love—God's kind of love—will defeat racism and hatred. Only God's light—the light of truth which is Jesus—will drive out the darkness. Our job as Christians is to love everyone regardless of skin color, political party, or any other group difference.

And we must pray. Pray for love to flow through us to others. Pray for others to receive that love. Pray for others to come to faith in Jesus and to be delivered from darkness, hatred, and racism. Pray for an end to the demonic ideologies that sow discord and disharmony. The voice of our prayers to God may be mightier than our voice of testimony to some people.

When we pray, we know God will hear and answer. Psalm 77:1 says, "I cried out to God with my voice, even to God with my voice; and He listened to me" (MEV).

1619 Project

Although critical race theory emerged in the 1990s, it has taken nearly thirty years to reach the point where it is today—a major threat to our way of life. Another new ideology stems from it and serves to enforce it—the 1619 project. Most have heard of its appearance in public schools and of the conflict between political parties over its implementation. Information about it abounds online.

Basically, it's a tool to rewrite our national history. It changes the date of the nation's birth from July 4, 1776 to 1619, the year that slaves first arrived on our shores. The project, enshrined in k-12 curriculum, views American history through the lens of slavery. It assigns the motive of preserving slavery as that motive through which the founders, in 1776, pledged to each other their lives, their fortunes, and their sacred honor.

Furthermore, it makes meaningless their "reliance on the protection of Divine Providence,"[5] since they had earlier stated that all men [people] "are created equal, that they are endowed by their Creator with certain unalienable rights, that among these are life, liberty, and the pursuit of happiness"[6]. If their main motive was to deny a race of people those God-given rights, they had no business relying on divine providence.

But to reaffirm critical race theory, history must read that preserving slavery was the motive behind the revolution, the basis upon which the country was founded, and the intention of whites from the beginning. This doesn't make sense, though. Out of the original thirteen colonies which formed the United States, only four states succeeded in the civil war. Only four out of thirteen fought to preserve slavery. The others were considered northern states from the beginning, and though slavery was allowed in the north, it ended more quickly there.

But the point is that knowledge of God, belief in Judeo-Christian principles and morals, and a dependence upon divine providence were key factors in the formation of our county. To assign the motive of ensuring slavery to our founders is to malign the brave men who sacrificed their lives and fortunes for our liberty. Personal freedom and religious beliefs drove them, not the preservation of the practice of enslaving Africans.

How would we feel if, one or two hundred years from now, our descendants assigned evil motives to the actions we are taking in the 21st century to care for our homeless and veterans, to protect our liberty, and to help developing nations?

The fact is that the 1619 project is rooted in hate. It assigns hateful and racist motives to people based on their skin color. It presumes that white people always act to oppress people of color. It assigns the motive of racism to everything white people do. And that, in itself, is racist.

And, as Dr. King said, "Hate cannot drive out hate; only love can do that." Love is how we combat these two evil ideologies. Love and our voices speaking the truth in love.

Love Drives out Hate

We must not embrace these errors. We must speak out against them as the Holy Spirit leads. At work, if assigned a training session where we are instructed to apologize for our inherent racism, we can speak of God's love, which transcends races. Christians who recognize signs of racism in themselves can ask for God's forgiveness and for power to change.

Additionally, we must find out if these are part of the curriculum at our children's schools and, if they are, we can homeschool or at least tell our children the truth after school. We can make sure our children are not learning racism from us. And we can work to clean up the curriculum. But we dare not ignore these errors. Silence only gives credence and strength to them.

We counter these with God's Word and with common sense. Galatians 3:28 and Romans 10:12–13 show that in the church, there is no difference between nationalities, ethnicities, races, or social standing. And in Acts 10:34–35, Peter states, "I see very clearly that God shows no favoritism. In every nation he accepts those who fear him and do what is right" (NLT). God is not interested in skin color. The words of Jesus in John 3:16 make it clear that God's love for humanity includes all races: "For God so loved the world" (KJV).

If we look at some of the current issues in the United States, we can see some humans showing an unfavorable opinion of people of color. The whole argument against voter ID is that it disenfranchises people of color because they can't get photo IDs. To think that a race of people are not able to get IDs is an insult to them and smacks of racism.

The same ones who make that argument are pushing critical race theory. So perhaps they are admitting to *their own* racism. But that doesn't make all whites racist, nor does it make all members of their political party racist. Just examining issues allows us to see the incongruity of their positions.

The Old Testament contains a command against removing the landmarks or boundaries of property. See Deuteronomy 19:14 and 27:17 and Proverbs 22:28 and 23:10. Hosea 5:10 says, "The princes of Judah have become like those who move a boundary; On them I will pour out My wrath like water" (NASB). Since Israel's kingdom was earthly and pertained to land, to move a boundary was like stealing an inheritance or changing ownership of the land—the heritage.

For us, our heritage is liberty—the rights and freedoms guaranteed by our founding documents. If we change the date, motive, and reason for the creation of our nation, we are, in essence, *moving the boundary.* And for that, wrath will fall like water. Of course, those who deny the Judeo-Christian influence on the founding fathers will scoff at this. But a close examination of historical documents and artifacts will reveal that biblical morality and a Christian worldview shaped the thoughts and actions of our founders.

Common sense would tell us that the founding of a nation is predicated on documents which attest to such intent. We have those documents in the 1774 Declaration of Independence and the 1787 Constitution. Are there documents from 1619 that show intent to form a nation separate from England or other European nations? No. How then does it make sense to assume that 1619 is the date of the founding of this nation? It doesn't make sense.

Furthermore, in 1774, the founders pledged their lives, their fortunes, and their sacred honor to the task at hand of winning independence from Britain. There was no such pledge, or anything close to a pledge, in 1619. To allow the 1619 project to become part of k-12 curriculum, with its erroneous assertions and racist conclusions, is *moving the boundary* and inviting disaster.

Response to These Errors

Sometimes, I can't resist sharing memes on Facebook that point out the hypocrisy and faults of those who want to destroy this nation and its biblical roots. Occasionally, I'll post a sarcastic quip before I check myself, and then discover that I started a hateful thread of comments. And this exposes my hypocrisy. I will never be able to share the love of Jesus with a tongue (or fingers) that spread disharmony. I will not convince the Christ-rejecters to face the truth about themselves while I am acting just like them. It will take love, not sarcasm.

And it will take love to combat racism, critical race theory, and the 1619 project.

The Key to Love

The key to loving others is to know how much Christ loves them—enough to die for them. And his love in us longs to reach out to them through us, inviting them into his family. Jesus wants to embrace the "political foe" we feel disgust for. He wants to spend eternity with the person who hates us because we're white or black or some other shade or color. Jesus wants fellowship with the woman who aborted her child, the person caught in homosexuality, the child plagued with gender confusion, and the lost souls in the culture who ignore truth and righteousness and chase after sin.

But that fellowship can only come as they acknowledge who he is and his right to set the terms. Faith in him as divine Son of God—Lord and Savior—brings relationship. Seeking truth and righteousness brings fellowship. And the closeness of an embrace comes as we walk with him, learn his Word, and let his love be our motivation and message. Our voice can bring victory to us and to others. If we speak the truth in love.

Agape Love

In Chapter 6, we discussed the Greek word that expresses God's love. This *agape* love does not compromise with sin. It is not a politically correct *tolerance* of sin, nor does it celebrate sin. Romans 12:9 makes this clear: "Let love be without hypocrisy. Abhor what is evil. Cling to what is good" (NKJV). God's love is pure, good, righteous, beneficial, productive, fruitful, and positive.

This love also corrects when correction is needed, just as a loving parent reprimands a wayward or disobedient child. At times, Jesus used what many would call harsh language today. (See Matthew 12:34 and 23:27–33.) Even John the Baptist called the hypocritical Pharisees a "brood of snakes" (Matthew 3:7 NLT).

Agape love is sometimes expressed by sharp rebuke. It is not always voiced in sweet tones of affirmation. We will know when to use reproach and when to use courtesy if we are walking in the Spirit and letting the love of God flow through us.

God's love brings redemption, salvation, deliverance, and sanctification. It produces joy, peace, and hope. And that's the kind of love that is to be "shed abroad in our hearts" (Romans 5:5 MEV). That's the kind of love that can speak truth when the culture demands silence. And it is what our culture needs to stamp out racism of all kinds, to preserve our heritage, and to build up the kingdom of God with new believers.

And that last point is the most important. How to turn "enemies" into friends—introduce them to Jesus so they will become a brother or sister in Christ by faith in him.

For more about God's love, visit my website for a free resource, "God's Surpassing Love," at victorythroughlight.com/freeresources.

Reflect Further

1. Read Romans 13:8–10; Galatians 5:13–14; 1 Thessalonians 3:12; 1 Peter 1:22; and 1 John 4:7–11, 19. Some of these Scriptures focus on loving fellow believers. However, Romans 5:8 tells us that God loved us while we were yet

sinners. Are we to love others before or only after they become Christians? Explain.

2. Does the death of Christ, motivated by love, inspire holy living or celebration of sin? What does *real* love look like?

3. How do we manifest both God's love and his righteousness when dealing with people whose lifestyle is abhorrent to God and disobedient to his Word?

4. Read Deuteronomy 16:19; 2 Chronicles 19:7; Proverbs 24:23; Acts 10:34–35; Romans 2:11; and James 2:9. Would you say that God is NOT racist? Would you say that he doesn't want us to be racist?

5. Read Ephesians 3:14–19. With what are we filled when we are "filled with all the fullness of God" (Ephesians 3:19 MEV)?

6. Read 1 Corinthians 16:14; 2 Timothy 2:22; 1 John 3:1, 11, 23; and 2 John 1:5–6. What benefits flow from being established in God's love? What responsibilities?

7. Read 1 Timothy 1:5. Agape love should come from "a pure heart, a clear conscience, and genuine faith" (NLT). Is this the kind of love that characterizes the politically correct (PC) culture? Do unbelievers understand this kind of love?

8. What other verses about love can you find from the Old and New Testaments? What do they say about the blessings and benefits of love? What responsibilities do they mention?

CHAPTER 11

Spiritual Fruit as Voice

WE STARTED THIS BOOK with stories and discussions about privatization, both voluntary and forced. We've worked our way through the various types of persecution used to silence us and hinder our message of life and truth.

We've learned that God's kind of love is to be our motivation, and we've seen how important it is to rightly define and correctly identify that love. We've studied how love is supposed to correct and bring people to repentance so that the righteousness of God will be seen in them. We've seen some of the current cultural attacks on love and learned that love can overcome them.

And now we come to the reality of how our lives most effectively will be a witness. It is not through self-effort, self-righteousness, or self-works that we will shine as light and speak truth in love. The epistles are full of instructions about yielding to the Lord, to righteousness, to the Spirit, and about ceasing old nature works and sins.

The apostles encourage us to live so as to please and glorify the Lord. When we are first born again, these things may seem unattainable, but as we learn to walk in the Spirit, obey the Word, and yield to Christ in us, we find ourselves growing and our faith increasing. This brings us joy and hope. But then the other shoe drops, so to speak.

The culture may reject us, scorn us, and tell us to keep silent about our faith. People we thought were friends may call us bigots or fanatics. We might hear of the so-called "violence gene" allegedly inherent in fundamentalists—folks who believe in the inerrancy of Scripture. With so much negativity bombarding us, how dare we speak?

How can we be light to a culture that chooses darkness and demands our silence? How can we grow in such a dark and confusing environment? Let's consider that process briefly.

There is a quotation often attributed to C. S. Lewis, which sums up the proper motive for letting our light shine, for walking in the Spirit and for letting the Holy Spirit produce good fruit in us: "Don't shine so others can see you. Shine so that through you, others can see Him." Thus, we should not focus on whether or not we're growing or being light or producing fruit. We focus on Christ and his Word, and the Spirit in us will produce the light and fruit. We cannot do this through self-effort.

Christ in Us

However, we can do this as Christ reigns in us. Paul explains this in Romans 5:17, 21:

> For if by one man's trespass death reigned through him, then how much more will those who receive abundance of grace and the gift of righteousness reign in life through the One, Jesus Christ. . . . so that just as sin reigned in death, grace might reign through righteousness unto eternal life through Jesus Christ our Lord. (MEV)

It takes Christ in us to live the way we should in this present world. Letting Christ live in us is also described as putting off the old creation and putting on the new. Read Ephesians 4:17—5:18 for a description of this. Verses 22–24 of Ephesians 4 explain more:

> [T]hrow off your old sinful nature and your former way of life, which is corrupted by lust and deception. Instead, let the Spirit renew your thoughts and attitudes. Put on your new nature, created to be like God—truly righteous and holy. (NLT)

The following verses explain how to do this. Read Ephesians 4: 25–32.

Ephesians 5 continues the discussion. Two of Paul's main instructions are to have a "life filled with love" (v. 2 NLT) and to "be filled with the Holy Spirit" (v. 18 NLT). Between those two verses, he cautions us to not be fooled by those who disobey God and participate in sin, and to not partake with them (vv. 6–7). And Paul reminds us, "For once you were full of darkness, but now you have light from the Lord. So live as people of light! Carefully determine what pleases the Lord" (vv. 8, 10 NLT).

No Compromise

This is clear. We are not to be swayed by the speech of the ungodly. We are not to compromise the light of truth for the darkness of sin. To allow rebellious and unrighteous practices into the pulpits and the positions of ministry in our churches is not scriptural. We can shout "love" all we want, but accepting and celebrating sin is not a response of agape love—it is a response of compromise, a result of deception, and a product of error and darkness.

We are to "take no part in the worthless deeds of evil and darkness; instead, expose them" (Ephesians 5:11 NLT). Note that we don't abandon the individual, but we refuse to associate with their sin. We reprove them of the sin which they do, but we do not condemn their soul. The person can come to church, but he or she should not be allowed in the pulpit or other place of responsibility as long as that sin is part of their life.

Who says if they're in sin? Simple. Judge according to the Word.

Over and over in Ephesians 5, Paul insists that we reject politically correct views and compromised practices of those who are not really saved or behaving scripturally. From this we can conclude that we are not to receive gay ministers or teachers in the church as leaders. They must first repent and leave that disobedient lifestyle. We are not to go along with gender confusion, transgendered rebels, adultery, and other practices of confusion, sin, and idolatry (self-worship).

Can believers be confused? Yes. But the response of love is to guide the confused person into accepting him or herself as God made them—scientifically, biologically, and factually. Feeding their confusion is not love but sabotage. It hastens their stumbling and encourages them to surrender to sin.

Notice that Paul also includes "greed" as something to avoid (Ephesians 5:3). We all know that greed is an extreme desire for money or possessions. Besides leading to theft, deception, or cheating as a means to gain money, greed as an attitude places things above God. Thus, it is idolatry. Definitely something we should not allow in our lives.

The so-called enlightened (or "woke") church, or "progressive" Christianity, is unscriptural and in opposition to God. Many individuals in that system are not born-again. The term used to be "nominal Christians"—Christians in name only. They validate many sins, hiding some and displaying others. To even talk about the activities which they conceal brings shame and disgust.

And today, they are doing some things openly with no attempt to hide the shameful conduct (such as ordaining gay and lesbian ministers). Instead, they expect us to hide our faith, as though it were shameful, to conceal the righteousness of God which is in us. However, we cannot and dare not do that, "For God has not called us to uncleanness, but to holiness" (1 Thessalonians 4:7 MEV).

Spiritual Growth

It takes growth in the Lord to mature to this point. By yielding to Christ in us and by walking in the Spirit, we can grow spiritually. Peter tells us to "grow in the grace and knowledge of our Lord and Savior Jesus Christ" (2 Peter 3:18 MEV). Yielding to the Holy Spirit fosters our growth in grace, and studying and believing the Word brings us to deeper knowledge.

The alternative for us is to stay a babe in Christ, learning nothing, taking no victories, being tossed to and fro by the world system, afraid to stand for Christ, compromising with the culture, and living in defeat. Read 1 Peter 2:2; 1 Corinthians 3:1–3; and Hebrews 5:12–14, all of which mention our spiritual nourishment through stages of growth.

God knows we start as babes, taking in the milk of the Word—the grace of God. He desires that we expand our knowledge of his Word and his will. That is like eating solid food. It comes as we yield more and more to him. And God desires that we grow "in every way more and more like

Christ" (Ephesians 4:15 NLT). This spiritual growth secures
for us the fruit of the Spirit.

Spiritual Fruit

We can't take credit for the fruit we bear if it is true spiritual
fruit. It is God's fruit—his characteristics—in us. We don't
make it appear. Just like when we garden. We may plant,
water, cultivate, remove weeds, fertilize, and tend our tomato
vines, picking off the horn worms and such, but the tomato
plant itself must bloom and then produce the fruit. Ultimately
God makes it happen by giving sunlight, nutrients in the soil,
and wind and bees to pollenate the blossoms. Eventually, we
harvest the ripe and tasty fruit.

Likewise, we cannot make spiritual fruit appear in us.
However, God will produce the fruit of the Spirit in us as we
yield to him and walk in the Spirit. The most familiar Scripture dealing with the fruit of the Spirit is found in Galatians 5.

In Galatians 5:19–21, the works of the flesh stand in sharp
contrast to the fruit of the Spirit. The flesh—the old creation
propensity to sin—produces works. There are eighteen listed
in these verses, the last of which comprises all sinful behav-
iors not listed in the other seventeen—"and other sins like
these" (v. 21 NLT).

A few verses earlier, Paul exhorts,

> So I say, let the Holy Spirit guide your lives. Then you
> won't be doing what your sinful nature craves. The sinful
> nature wants to do evil, which is just the opposite of what
> the Spirit wants. And the Spirit gives us desires that are the
> opposite of what the sinful nature desires. These two forces
> are constantly fighting each other, so you are not free to
> carry out your good intentions. (vv. 16–17 NLT).

Paul describes this tug-of-war in great detail in Romans 7. The important thing to remember is that our old nature, which God counts as dead, cannot bear good fruit. It can only produce sinful works.

The way to keep it from producing sinful works is for us to walk in the Spirit—to let the Lord lead us by the Holy Spirit, and to live in obedience to Christ and to his Word.

Belonging to Christ means that we have crucified our old nature—the flesh—with its passions and lusts and are now living in the spiritual realm guided by the Holy Spirit. We do indeed "live in the Spirit," and can also then "walk in the Spirit" (Galatians 5:25 MEV). Other verses that express this idea are Romans 6:4–8, 11–13, 21–22; 2 Corinthians 5:17; and Galatians 2:20.

Fruit of the Spirit

Thus, the fruit of the Spirit will be produced in us as we yield to the Spirit, walk in the Spirit, and live in the Spirit. The Spirit brings forth the fruit. It is a nine-fold fruit: "love, joy, peace, patience, gentleness, goodness, faith, meekness, and self-control" (Galatians 5:22–23 MEV). These are all things which are not forbidden by any law, especially the Mosaic Law.

With the right training and effort, some people can mimic these qualities. We all know people who seem loving, joyous, gentle, and able to control their tempers and such. Some of those people may even be nonbelievers. But the positive qualities produced by the old creation have limits and flaws. It takes a true work of the Holy Spirit in the life of a Christian to produce the fruit of the Spirit as listed in Galatians 5. A brief discussion follows.

Love

The first facet of this fruit is agape love, of which we've spoken in earlier chapters. As we have seen, we are to speak the truth in love and to show love to those whose actions we must rebuke. This is not a work that we must do through our self-effort. It is a fruit that God produces in us. In that way, it truly is agape love—God's love through us to others.

Romans 5:5 speaks of this: "because the love of God is shed abroad in our hearts by the Holy Spirit who has been given to us" (MEV). This kind of love is what Stephen exhibited when he asked God to forgive those who were stoning him to death. It is the love that Jesus showed to those who crucified him. It is the love we are called upon to let blossom into fruit in our lives, in whatever situation or circumstance the Lord brings our way.

Jesus commands us to "love one another" (John 13:34 NKJV) and to love our enemies (Matthew 5:44). Loving our enemies is difficult. That's why we need the fruit of the Spirit. The Spirit can enable us to love the unlovely, to love the unlovable, and to love those who hate us.

Joy

The next fruit, joy, carries us through the times of persecution. Remember how the disciples responded to persecution in the early chapters of Acts. In Acts 5:41, we see that they rejoiced to be "counted worthy to suffer shame for his name" (KJV). Rejoicing expresses joy. Joy enabled Paul and Silas, having been beaten and chained in the deepest dungeon, to pray and sing praises to God (Acts 16:25).

Jesus wants us to have joy. In John 15:11, he says, "These things have I spoken unto you, that my joy might remain in you, and that your joy might be full" (KJV). Again in John 16:24 he says, "Hitherto have ye asked nothing in my name: ask, and ye shall receive, that your joy may be full" (KJV). And in John 17:13, part of his prayer is that "they might have my joy fulfilled in themselves" (KJV).

John, writing to churches of Asia near the end of the first century A. D., says, "And these things write we unto you, that your joy may be full" (1 John 1:4 KJV). What does "full joy" look like? It is joy that the Holy Spirit produces in us totally independent of circumstances.

I remember when I struggled as a single mom, working part-time and going to college full-time, fairly broke, and dependent on charity to pay medical bills when my son broke his arm falling out of a tree. I had no vehicle, and I was receiving surplus food via the Salvation Army.

I had every reason to feel discouraged and to wallow in despair. Stepping from the library one day, I felt an overwhelming joy flow through me. I couldn't stop the joy from overflowing in my heart and soul. My spirit rejoiced because of the Holy Spirit's work and fruit-bearing. A friend asked me why I smiled all the time when I should be moping around. I knew that I couldn't have produced the joy myself. I knew it was fruit of the Spirit, so I had an opportunity to witness.

No doubt, you have experienced this joy also, or known someone who has. This kind of joy encourages others, lifts those who are hurting, and brings victory to those in despair. It brings hope to the hopeless. Nehemiah declares that "the joy of the LORD is your strength" (Nehemiah 8:10 MEV).

Peace

Related to joy is peace. This spiritual fruit enables us to trust the Lord for all things—for our needs, for good to come of trouble, for ultimate victory over all enemies and obstacles. We have peace with God, the peace of God, and peace with one another. The Triune God gives us peace in the midst of any storm that rages around us.

Jesus calmed the stormy sea by commanding it, "Peace, be still" (Mark 4:39 MEV). Later, he tells the disciples, "Peace I leave with you. My peace I give to you. Not as the world gives do I give to you. Let not your heart be troubled, neither let it be afraid" (John 14:27 MEV). That same night—the night in which he was betrayed—he spoke other words of comfort: "I have told you these things so that in Me you may have peace. In the world you will have tribulation. But be of good cheer. I have overcome the world" (John 16:33 MEV).

As long as we abide in him, we can have peace. It is both a gift from him and a fruit that the Holy Spirit produces in us. We can have a peace that "surpasses all understanding" (Philippians 4:7 NKJV), which stabilizes us and keeps us calmly trusting the Lord in all things. The Holy Spirit produces this peace in our lives. That peace works through us toward others, so that we can live in peace with both believers and those who are not yet in the family of God. See Hebrews 12:14 and Romans 12:18.

Thus, if our government tells us that we cannot hold church services or sing during worship, or that we must wear masks in public, we can have peace. If a political party rises to power and abuses that power to alter this blessed nation from a republic to a socialistic third-world country, we can have peace. As long as we look at things eternal, not things temporal, we can have peace.

Patience

So far the fruit is sweet and attractive. Who wouldn't want to produce and to experience love, joy, and peace? However, patience comes next. We all know what that looks like and what it looks like to *lose one's patience*. We've all been there and done that.

The Greek word used means more than human patience with the limitations of others (like toilet training a toddler or being stuck behind a slow driver). It includes patient endurance of injuries, hardships, offenses, or troubles, with forbearance. Persistent tenacity.

The King James Version translates the word as "longsuffering," which is basically *suffering long*. It includes an acceptance of difficulties and rejoicing in them. Jesus set the example in the garden of Gethsemane when he prayed, "Father, if You are willing, remove this cup from Me. Nevertheless not My will, but Yours, be done" (Luke 22:42 MEV). He was willing to patiently endure what he must for the desired outcome.

The Holy Spirit uses our hardships and persecutions, our trials and tests, to produce in us the fruit of patience. James speaks of this:

> My brethren, count it all joy when you fall into various trials, knowing that the testing of your faith produces patience. But let patience have its perfect work, that you may be perfect and complete, lacking nothing. (James 1:2-4 NKJV)

Indeed we can accept adversities and difficulties if we know they are working fruit of the Spirit in us.

Gentleness

Gentleness follows, translated *kindness* or *goodness* in some versions. The Greek word alludes to moral excellence in character or demeanor, and its root word suggests being useful or employed regarding manners or morals. So, it is more than just displaying an outward show of thoughtfulness or benevolence.

This aspect of the spiritual fruit comes from an attitude of personal responsibility to work and to help others. It springs from a belief in being responsible to God to treat others as he does—with agape love and brotherly kindness. We have a moral responsibility to work and to fulfill the duties appropriate to our role, and the Holy Spirit gives us the gentleness to do just that. And for those who are stay-at-home moms, as you know, being a homemaker is work. Don't let our culture intimidate you into thinking that you are not performing a valuable vocation.

Even while boasting of God's instruction in warfare, David writes, "You have given me the shield of Your salvation, and Your right hand has held me up, and Your gentleness has made me great" (Psalm 18:35 MEV). David declares that God's gentleness—not might or courage or military prowess—has made him great. That same gentleness can work in us.

Gentleness is not permissiveness. True, godly gentleness does not stand by and allow sin, rebellion, and disobedience to run rampant when it is in the realm of our responsibility to control such behavior. For example, it does not mean that, as parents, we are to let our children run loose. We should not exercise a fake "gentleness" and allow them to wreck havoc in public or at home.

The apostle Paul pleads with the Corinthians, "Now I Paul myself beseech you by the meekness and gentleness of Christ," (2 Corinthians 10:1 KJV), therein affirming that our Lord indeed is gentle and meek as well as strong and mighty. Paul followed that pattern, stating that "we were gentle among you" (1 Thessalonians 2:7 KJV). And in Titus 3:2, Paul instructs Titus to remind the believers "to speak evil of no one, not to be contentious, but gentle, showing all humility toward everyone" (MEV).

Thus, we are all expected to show gentleness. But we cannot produce it by self-effort. It does not spring from the old creation. The fruit of gentleness comes only from the Holy Spirit working in us.

Goodness

Next is goodness—a Greek word denoting intrinsic goodness, virtue, or beneficence. Thus, the innate goodness which characterizes God and is ours by faith. When we are born again, we become a new creation, and this attribute is ours. We let it be obvious and manifest in our lives by walking in the Spirit and bearing the fruit of the Spirit.

Goodness is seeking the well-being of others. In the Old Testament, the word is akin to mercy (Psalm 33:5) and often linked with mercy (Psalm 23:6). In Romans 2:4, we see that God's goodness is what leads us to repentance. There, Paul writes, "Do you despise the riches of His goodness, tolerance, and patience, not knowing that the goodness of God leads you to repentance?" (MEV). God's goodness in offering us salvation by grace moves us to accept him by faith.

Then his goodness can be produced in our lives by the Holy Spirit. Through that goodness, we will draw others to the Lord. We need only yield to God and let the fruit of goodness appear as we live and walk in the Spirit.

Faith

Next is faith. The Greek word suggests persuasion, credence, conviction of religious truth, reliance upon Christ for salvation, and being constant in that belief. It is the system of religious and spiritual truth which governs our lives. For the Christian, it is biblical truth—the gospel.

It includes assurance, fidelity, and belief. We have a "full assurance of faith" that the gospel is true (Hebrews 10:22 KJV). We are faithful to the Lord as he is to us. We believe God's Word and rest in him. That is the essence of faith.

So, then, what is faith as a fruit of the Spirit? By faith we accept God's Word as true, acknowledge our sin and need of the Savior, and embrace his provision. It's the means by which we are saved. However, as we yield to him and walk in the Spirit, that faith grows in us and produces the fruit of more faith. Our faith increases. At first, it is the size of a mustard seed. But Jesus assures us that is enough. See Matthew 17:20 and Luke 17:5–6.

How does faith grow? By hearing the Word (Romans 10:17). So it stands to reason that the more Word we hear, the more we will grow in both knowledge and faith. That is one way we exercise faith. As we see God rescuing and providing for his people throughout the Bible, our faith in his sovereign providence for us will increase. The other way we exercise our faith is simply to believe God in tough situations. By the end of the trial, our faith will be stronger. But it takes the Holy Spirit to work this in us.

Our experience of faith—like that of love, joy, peace, patience, gentleness, goodness, meekness, and self-control—should continually expand and grow. And it will if we live in the Spirit, walk in the Spirit, and let the Spirit produce his fruit in us.

Meekness

The Greek word translated meekness implies *gentleness* and *humility*. It is calm patience combined with quiet courage and sympathetic love. In our current culture, with the redefinition of many words and ideas, meekness carries a negative connotation of being overly and unduly submissive.

However, the biblical definition of the word lacks that connotation. Instead, it carries a positive connotation—to be meek is good and brings blessings. Moses was called "meek," as was Jesus (Numbers 12:3 KJV; Matthew 11:29 KJV).

Some versions translate "meek" as "humble." Both David and Jesus said that the meek will inherit the earth (Psalm 37:11 KJV; Matthew 5:5 KJV). That is foreign to today's culture and to all humanity, which sees power and pride as the way to positions of control.

But meekness is not weakness. It is the opposite of hubris, which is a false pride in self that springs from narcissistic self-idolization. We should seek to manifest the fruit of meekness and "not be conceited, provoking one another and envying one another" (Galatians 5:26 MEV). Meekness repels envy and jealousy. It attracts humility and contentment.

The meek are open to the gospel (Psalm 76:9 KJV; Isaiah 61:1 KJV; and Zephaniah 2:3 KJV). And spiritual leaders should be meek (Galatians 6:1 KJV; 2 Corinthians 10:1 KJV). Meekness compels us to speak the truth in love.

Self-control

The final aspect of the fruit of the Spirit is self-control, also translated *temperance*. This is often thought of as continence or self-control. Some may find this thought strange, that self-control would be a fruit of the Spirit rather than an effort or work of the flesh. It does take some effort to exercise self-control. One must be able to say "no" to temptation.

We can look at King David's life and conclude that he was short on self-control regarding his attraction to Bathsheba. Or we could point to Amnon and proclaim that he lacked self-control regarding his half-sister Tamar. And what about Samson, who kept falling for Philistine women? How different their testimonies would have been if they had exercised self-control!

Are we to conclude that there are no biblical examples of self-control or temperance? No. Look at Joseph regarding Potiphar's wife (Genesis 39:6–12). Her false accusation of him ensured his imprisonment, but had he given in to temptation, he would have deserved that imprisonment—and ruined his testimony.

The core of self-control is to use self-restraint in matters of chastity. The temperate person controls sexual desires and responses to those desires. They are not promiscuous, nor are they given to excess in substances such as alcohol. Self-control enables us to maintain a healthy lifestyle.

When confronted by Paul, the Roman politician Felix trembled at the mention of "righteousness, self-control, and the coming judgment" (Acts 24:25 MEV). Why? Felix was neither righteous nor self-controlled, and he was subject to judgment as a Christ-rejecter.

Having self-control is a quality necessary to be a bishop (Titus 1:8 NKJV). And anyone who seeks to excel in any sport or activity, or to achieve a worthy goal, must exercise self-control (1 Corinthians 9:25).

Our old creation nature either recoils from self-control and pursues over-indulgence or indulges in self-restraint to the point of being legalistic and self-righteous. But true self-control is a godly characteristic that results from the new creation life in us. It is perfected by the Holy Spirit in us and springs forth as fruit. And there is no law against spiritual fruit (Galatians 5:23).

In Romans 6:13, we're told to not yield to sin, but to yield to God:

> Do not yield your members to sin as instruments of un-righteousness, but yield yourselves to God, as those who are alive from the dead, and your bodies to God as instruments of righteousness. (MEV)

This takes self-control on our part. God doesn't make us puppets. We must have the inner discipline to say "no" to sin and "yes" to God. And we need the Holy Spirit to produce in us that self-control.

Quality Fruit

The kind of fruit produced in our lives is determined by whom or what we yield to. If to sin, we reap a harvest of sin, uncleanness, defilement, and death—the works of the flesh. (See Galatians 5:16–21.) If to God, then fruit of holiness. (See Romans 6:22.) Hence, producing the fruit of the Spirit is a matter of yielding to God, living and walking in the Spirit, and serving God's righteousness. It is how we speak to our culture without saying a word.

These qualities of the fruit of the Spirit appear in various combinations in other Scriptures. In 2 Peter 1:4, Peter refers to these qualities as "the divine nature" of which we, as born-again believers, are made "partakers." As children of God by faith, we actually partake of his divine nature and can exhibit the characteristics of our Lord. Peter lists these in verses 5–8:

> For this reason make every effort to add virtue to your faith; and to your virtue, knowledge; and to your knowledge, self-control; and to your self-control, patient endurance; and to your patient endurance, godliness; and to your godliness, brotherly kindness; and to your brotherly kindness, love. For if these things reside in you and abound, they ensure that you will neither be useless nor unfruitful in the knowledge of our Lord Jesus Christ. (MEV)

What if a believer lacks these things? Peter says, "But the one who lacks these things is blind and shortsighted because he has forgotten that he was cleansed from his former sins" (2 Peter 1:9 MEV).

So, it is possible to be born again but not produce or exhibit the fruit of the Spirit. When we forget that we have escaped "the world's corruption caused by human desires" (2 Peter 1:4 NLT), we follow the urges of our old creation nature, producing the works of the flesh. (See Galatians 5:19–21.)

Often, bearing fruit is the only testimony we can give in the midst of a culture that demands silence. We cannot always speak of the blood of the cross and of salvation by grace through faith. But we can show forth the fruit of the Spirit as our witness of the reality of our faith. As the adage says, "Actions speak louder than words."

Satan's Substitute

However, we must be prepared for Satan's substitutes for fruit of the Spirit. Postmodernism has brought to our culture new qualities that unbelievers (and some shallow believers) value more than the fruit of the Spirit. We've talked about these earlier in this book, and I cover some of them in *Victory through Light: How to Overcome the Growing Cultural Darkness.*

These faux virtues include relative morality; gender diversity and dysphoria; a redefined tolerance which validates former taboos; inclusivism (not of people but of ideas and religious practices); syncretism of religious ideas into pluralism; political correctness to the extreme; identity politics as replacement for character; humanistic globalism; critical race theory; and even environmentalism (including climate change).

While some of these are not bad in themselves (such as tolerance, rightly defined, and caring for the environment), their importance is exaggerated. But in the toxic culture prevalent today, lining up one's words and thoughts with these cultural values is expected—even demanded, at the risk of being "canceled."

If we think differently, we are forced to be silent, privatize our beliefs, and acquiesce to these. The penalty for noncompliance is to be publicly shamed, driven out of business or terminated from employment, and placed on various blacklists. The secular culture regards these faux values more than the real virtues of a godly life, expressed by the fruit of the Spirit.

Love Plus the Fruit of the Spirit

Therefore, we must speak the truth in love, whatever the cost. Additionally, if we also show real love and concern for others, our actions will speak loudly enough to get their attention. And as we've said, real love does not validate bad choices or sin, but it loves the person in spite of their bad choices or sin. Real love seeks a positive change and eternal good for the person.

Furthermore, if we get their attention with the fruit of the Spirit in evidence, perhaps they will listen to our words, spoken in love, that can bring them deliverance, redemption, and eternal life.

This is letting our light shine, as Jesus says in Matthew 5:16: "Let your light so shine before men, that they may see your good works, and glorify your Father which is in heaven" (KJV). Actions do speak louder than words, and the fruit of the Spirit produces godly actions that speak truth even when the culture demands silence.

Reflect Further

1. Read Mark 4:7–8, 14–20. What are the thorns, if any, in your life that might be hindering fruit-bearing? Do you want to bear thirty, sixty, or one-hundred fold?

2. Read Matthew 7:16–18; 12:33; and Luke 6:43–45. Since Jesus states in Mark 10:18 that there is none good but God, can we conclude that a "good man" is one who is born again and has Christ living in them? Can we conclude that an "evil man" is one who has rejected Christ and chosen darkness and sin, who lives only by the power of the fallen old nature? What is your understanding of the verses from Matthew 7 and 12 and Luke 6, in light of this?

3. Read Luke 13:6–9. Jesus didn't explain that parable as he did other parables. What do you think it means? Does digging the soil and fertilizing the tree represent trials and persecutions, which could make the tree bear fruit,

just as in a garden we might plant? Can persecution work in our favor, if it is necessary for fruit bearing? Can we expect to be "cut down" if we refuse to bear fruit? And what does that mean?

4. Read John 15:1–8. Looking at John 15, can we conclude that fruitfulness is conditioned on our dwelling in Christ and yielding to Christ in us? What happens to a believer who fails to draw his strength from Christ (v. 6)? Since Jesus says, "men gather them and cast them into the fire" (KJV), can we conclude that God does not cast them away, but that people do? Do you know of any prominent Christians (or not so prominent), whose lives and actions have betrayed their profession and brought shame to the gospel? Must we be on guard lest it happen to us?

5. Read 2 Corinthians 9:10 and Philippians 1:11. In these Scriptures, we read of "fruits of righteousness." How do these differ from acts of self-righteousness? See Matthew 6:1; Isaiah 64:6; and Philippians 3:9.

6. Read 2 Samuel 12:13–14. If we bring forth bad fruit (works of the flesh), we do not lose salvation. That is evident in the life of King David. However, what is the result to our testimony and the effect upon the culture? (See Titus 2:5, 8, 10.)

7. Read Habakkuk 3:17–18 and 1 Thessalonians 1:6. Can joy thrive in spite of troubles and afflictions? Have you experienced this kind of joy?

8. Read Matthew 5:9. What does it mean to be a peace-maker? Do you need to have peace in order to be a peacemaker? Does this take the Holy Spirit's intervention?

9. Read 2 Corinthians 12:7–10. Paul's conclusion (v. 10) expresses victory. Do you think Paul needed the Holy Spirit to work that patience and long-suffering into his experience and make him willing to bear the affliction? Can the Holy Spirit do the same for you if necessary?

CHAPTER 12

Speaking Foundational Truth

WE CAN PROCLAIM TRUTH with our words, deeds, or fruit. However, many believers sadly lack a full understanding of what that truth is. Because of the postmodern deconstruction of language and meaning, our culture has lost sight of the fact that there is one Truth that governs us all. That one Truth is Jesus Christ, who is "the way, the truth, and the life" (John 14:6 KJV).

Instead, the culture has grasped at many truths, individualized truths, truths that depend upon identity politics and political correctness—so-called truths that are not true at all.

Thus, we conclude with this chapter outlining the Truth which we are to proclaim (in love) to a culture that demands our silence. The self-appointed secular leaders in the culture demand our silence because they do not want the truth we proclaim. To accept it means they must acknowledge God, confess their sin, and repent of their ways. And, sadly, they have chosen darkness, just as Jesus said in John 3:19–21:

> This is the verdict, that light has come into the world, and men loved darkness rather than light, because their deeds

were evil. For everyone who does evil hates the light and does not come to the light, lest his deeds should be exposed. But he who does the truth comes to the light, that it may be revealed that his deeds have been done in God. (MEV)

As a result of their choice, they abhor our message and demand our silence. But we have seen that we cannot remain silent. Our lives and our voices must speak truth in love. However, believers must know the truth in order to speak it. And the sad thing is that many don't really know the foundational truth of the gospel.

Consequently, they may compromise righteousness and truth in the name of a redefined "love" that isn't really agape love at all. They may build their worldview on one or two verses removed from context and without respect to word meanings in the original language. Churches whose pastors fail to study the Word may quickly lose sight of what the gospel really is. This lack of basic biblical understanding hinders the proclamation of truth. It dims our light and muffles our voice.

Furthermore, this lack of understanding is widespread in the United States. In a blog on the Patheos.com website, Grayson Gilbert says,

[T]he majority of professing Christians do not believe that salvation is by grace through faith alone. While it might be alarming to some, it ought not to be a shock to us that the majority of professing Christians don't know the gospel . . . [and] have little to no concept of what the gospel actually teaches about the fundamental nature of mankind, the problem of sin and judgment, and yet how this problem is also resolved in the person and work of Jesus Christ.[1]

When it is essential to salvation to understand the fallen nature of man (original sin), how can salvation be understood without that knowledge? If sin is disallowed as a reality, and no judgment for disbelief is to be expected, then what is there to be saved from? And yet many professing Christians discount sin and claim that a good God would not send anyone to hell. This reduces the gospel to a set of rules to keep in order to earn heaven on one's own merit and to (hopefully, but impossibly) make society better.

Of this, Gilbert says, "What we are dealing with, in a nutshell, is a worldview competition, with the secular worldview emerging as the dominant one."[2] He contrasts the "truth of the Christian worldview" with a "cultural Christian worldview," which is different from the "atheistic worldview."[3]

Cultural Christian Worldview

Indeed, the *cultural Christian* worldview is the atheistic worldview with a splash of Christianity, but it fails to answer the basic questions of origin, truth, morality, and destiny. A cultural Christian worldview often lacks the understanding of several key points:

- the Triune God as Creator and sustainer;
- the fall of man into sin and, hence, the need of a Savior;
- the righteousness of God as our moral standard, and his right to set that standard; and
- the reality of an eternal destiny based on one's belief in the Redeemer, Jesus Christ, or a different destiny based upon one's rejection of that Savior.

Why does the cultural Christian worldview lack these basic anchors? Because it has compromised with the culture which asserts the contrary. The secular culture claims

- that the world and all we see is a product of evolution;

- that the concept of sin is outdated and that the only requirement for morality is "love," which the culture has redefined into something that isn't really love;
- that each person can decide what is right or wrong for him or herself (relative morality); and
- that there isn't such a thing as hell and that if a person is basically good, they'll pass into the light (i.e., heaven) when they die.

Additionally, they may see all people (including atheists) as "children of God," based on a creation that they often deny in favor of naturalistic evolution.

So where is the "Christianity" part of that incongruent and syncretic worldview? Well, there is the acknowledgement of the principle of "love," the existence of right and wrong, and a somewhat watered-down eternal home or destiny. Foundational to that worldview is the idea of a divine being called God, who is seen as a Father who loves all people. Often the cultural Christian denies that Jesus died for all who believe, because they see no need for the atonement for sin since they deny the existence of sin.

Unfortunately, those with a cultural Christian worldview fail to see that the real "children of God" are those who have been born again by faith in Christ or by the expectant belief in the Messiah, as in the days before Christ's birth. All others either have chosen condemnation (John 3:19–20) or have yet to accept Jesus as Savior.

Gilbert notes that this "piecemeal spirituality" embraced by many Christians fails to qualify as a true Christian worldview. Instead, it "is an amalgamation of clashing worldviews that people don't realize are in direct competition of one another, namely because professing Christians don't have a vigorously consistent worldview."⁴ Their worldview has become corrupted by a culture that is more interested in social identities, systemic oppression, and critical race theory.

To call this a *social gospel* misses the full extent of the departure from the fundamentals of the faith. This new *social gospel* goes beyond merely helping the poor or lifting them from poverty. It blames certain demographics for the plight of the poor, based on their skin color (white), their economic standing (middle class), their gender (male), and, broadly, their religious affiliation (Christian).

This is either a discipleship issue—just poor teaching in churches—or a knowing rejection of a comprehensive Christian worldview which is based on the inerrancy of the Bible. Indeed, Gilbert writes, "proper discipleship still demands a comprehensive biblical worldview born out of the gospel."⁵ However, many people today claim that the church should fulfill a social gospel and not focus on preaching the real gospel. The message of the cross, they claim, alienates people. It is seen as judgmental. Its doctrine of salvation by the shed blood of Jesus Christ is violent and offensive, they assert.

And this from professing Christians!

From Christians who should value all lives equally, regardless of color. Who should see every Christian as a brother or sister in Christ, and every non-Christian as a potential brother or sister with whom they should share the gospel. But because we've gotten sidelined into social issues, including race, we've grown silent about the essential eternal message.

Transformation of the Culture

Consequently, our culture is rapidly being transformed. Its Judeo-Christian roots are being cut off and replaced by secular humanism and all it represents, including its source, the devil. The only way to stop this cultural transformation is for believers to be transformed by the renewing of their minds, into the very image of Christ, and to stand for truth, shine as light, and speak the Word of God with love in the midst of the sin and sickness of the darkening culture.

When did this vacuum begin? Without going into a deep discussion of church history, briefly we can look at what happened in the United States in the 19th and 20th centuries. The 19th century modernists rejected and distorted certain doctrines, accepted Darwinism, and rejected the literal happening of miracles.

As a result, the fundamentalist movement in the late 19th and early 20th centuries restored the doctrine of the inerrancy of the Bible. Several different movements sprang from this, but tossing out the liturgy of the ancient creeds appears to be a commonality among them.

Though they stressed five core beliefs, without adequate teaching and the recitation of the core beliefs, the ordinary church member was left without a firm foundation, and over time, many fell to the compromises and errors of the modernists. The five main points were

1. the inerrancy of the Bible;
2. the literal nature of biblical accounts, including miracles and creation as in Genesis;
3. the virgin birth of Christ;

4. the bodily resurrection of Christ and his coming physical return; and

5. the substitutionary atonement provided by Christ through his death on the cross.

The Ancient Creeds

The ancient creeds, such as the Nicene and the Apostles' Creeds, delineated more than these five points. Some churches still honor and recite the creeds, particularly the Catholic Church and some of the protestant liturgical churches (Lutheran, Anglican/Episcopal, Presbyterian, and Greek Orthodox). However, the trend is increasingly away from recitation every Sunday, as was done in the mid-20th century.

I remember growing up Lutheran and learning the creeds and their explanations as part of catechism class, which was necessary in order to be allowed to partake of communion. I am grateful for that foundation I received. It helped me to more fully learn biblical truth and solid doctrine when, as an adult, I yielded to the Lord. My memory tells me that in my childhood church, we recited a creed every Sunday.

I did an informal query of my Facebook friends to see which churches might still recite either of the ancient creeds on a regular basis. It seems the Nicene Creed is regularly recited in some Catholic services. Among fundamentalists and evangelicals, the creeds are rarely recited, spoken about, or taught.

William D. Watkins, an award-winning author, editor, and president of Literary Solutions, reports that when he teaches Christian doctrines in Sunday school, middle school, or at the college level, he does draw "attention to the Apostles' Creed and the Nicene Creed. The latter especially when it comes to unpacking the Christian doctrine of the Incarnation."[6] This kind of training is important to establish believers in the sound doctrine of the Word of God.

The full value of understanding the points of the creeds cannot be underestimated. Watkins further states,

> From my experience in many evangelical churches, denominational or not, I've found the ancient creeds rarely used, much less accurately understood. Churches cut off from their ancient historical roots are easy targets for poor and false teaching, but even many Christian leaders don't seem to grasp that point.[7]

Foundational Truth

In order to grow in knowledge and become grounded in the faith, it is necessary to understand the foundational truths expressed in the ancient creeds. Now we know that Jesus himself is the Truth, as he says in John 14:6, "I am the way, the truth, and the life. No one comes to the Father except through Me" (NKJV). Thus, ultimately we proclaim Christ. But wrapped up in him is a whole system of truth—a worldview that is both coherent within itself and consistent with reality.

The truth which we proclaim bears several descriptive names. In Jude 1:3, we read of "the faith that God has entrusted once for all time to his holy people" (NLT). There, the word "faith" means the system of gospel truth itself as the basis of our reliance upon Christ for salvation.

Paul declares, "For I am not ashamed of the gospel of Christ, for it is the power of God to salvation for everyone who believes" (Romans 1:16 NKJV). He echoes this in 1 Corinthians 1:18: "For the preaching of the cross is to them that perish foolishness; but unto us which are saved it is the power of God" (KJV). The gospel is truth and, as such, is the power of God to save those who believe.

Paul gives us a hint of its scope in 2 Timothy 3:16–17:

> All Scripture is given by inspiration of God, and is profitable for doctrine, for reproof, for correction, for instruction in righteousness, that the man of God may be complete, thoroughly equipped for every good work. (NKJV)

The whole Word of God is the system of faith which we must defend and share with others. But we cannot share what we do not understand. Thus, having an understanding of the Word and its doctrine is essential to our testimony and witness. How can we speak the truth in love if we don't know the truth?

Points of the Creeds

The Apostles' Creed can be broken into twelve points of truth. The Nicene Creed expands upon these points, and adds language that references our salvation as the reason that Jesus, the Son, came down from heaven. It also adds an explanation that the Holy Spirit is worshipped as one with the Father and Son, and that he spoke through the prophets.

A Google search or a glance through liturgical hymnals will yield the text of these creeds for your in-depth study, if you wish. Certain words may vary depending on the denomination. Additionally, some churches still use King James English, while others use current verb forms. And some capitalize the first letter of major nouns.

The Apostles' Creed, divided into its twelve traditional points, follows:

1. I believe in God the Father Almighty, Maker of heaven and earth.
2. And in Jesus Christ, His only Son, our Lord;

3. who was conceived by the Holy Ghost, born of the Virgin Mary;

4. suffered under Pontius Pilate, was crucified, dead, and buried.

5. He descended into hell; the third day He rose again from the dead;

6. He ascended into heaven and sits on the right hand of God the Father Almighty;

7. from thence He shall come to judge the quick and the dead.

8. I believe in the Holy Ghost;

9. the holy Catholic [universal] Church, the communion of saints;

10. the forgiveness of sins;

11. the resurrection of the body; and

12. the life everlasting.

Note that these outline basic doctrines of who our Triune God is and how he has worked and will work in behalf of humanity. However, the creeds do not explain the truths of our personal relationship with the Father and the Son, our walk in the Spirit and his fruit in us, and the power of the gospel to change lives and cultures. Nor do they express the commission that we have to evangelize—to share these truths of salvation to all the world—to not be silenced.

Lausanne Covenant

In July, 1974, a group of evangelists, ministers, and scholars met to construct a mutual covenant that would express the hearts of Christians of all denominations. The well-renowned Billy Graham was there, working with the chief architect,

John Stott. It is basically a confession of faith, affirming the beliefs stated in the Nicene Creed and expressing the commission of world evangelization.[8]

Ministries, churches, and writers may agree to this covenant, but it isn't taught or recited in regular church services. It may be taught in seminaries, but that teaching does not generally trickle down to the pew sitters, whom Jesus calls upon to shine as light and to hold forth the Word of Life. Raised under the creeds, I didn't hear of the Lausanne Covenant until I attended a writers' conference in 2013 and found that many Christian publishers required their writers to agree to it.

We can only hope that ministers and denominations which subscribe to the covenant will teach and preach accordingly—with a balanced and scriptural emphasis upon the truths of the Word of God as summarized in the creeds. Its text can be found at lausanne.org/content/covenant/lausanne-covenant#cov.

The Lausanne Covenant includes a section that affirms the truth that there is only one Savior, Jesus Christ, and that we must reject all forms of syncretism, which claims or implies that Christ speaks in all religions and that all religions will lead to heaven. There is only "one mediator between God and men, the man Christ Jesus" (1 Timothy 2:5 KJV). Furthermore, "Neither is there salvation in any other: for there is none other name under heaven given among men, whereby we must be saved" (Acts 4:12 KJV). Thus, the covenant discusses a depth of relationship which the creeds do not.

However, the covenant, like the creeds, as valuable as they are, does not express the essential truths of the two natures (old and new) of the believer; the guarantee of eternal security in Christ; the high call of God for believers to be prepared as a spiritual bride for Jesus Christ; and the dispensational purpose of God to once again deal with his chosen people, Israel. With its emphasis on the universal church with its destiny in heaven, it omits the earthly destiny of Israel.

Ten Points of Essential Gospel Truth

As a brief overview of the "whole counsel of God" (Acts 20:27 MEV), I have created a list of ten points of essential gospel truth. A free resource, "Ten Essential Truths," is available on my website. It discusses these ten points in detail. The teaching adheres to the points of the creeds and covenant, but it expands upon certain doctrinal truths not specifically mentioned in the creeds or covenant.

For your further study, there are suggested readings and review questions at the end of that document. You may access it at victorythroughlight.com/freeresources. I do not offer it as a "new" creed to replace the others, but as a set of truths we should know for a comprehensive Christian worldview.

In that study, my goal is to present the gospel as God intends us to experience it, so that we can speak it in love to our hurting culture. Briefly, the ten points are these:

1. The Triune God created all that is, was, or ever will be.
2. Sin entered the world by man's disobedience and passed to all humans.
3. God sovereignly provided for mankind throughout the ages.
4. Born of a virgin, Christ came and lived among us as a man, working miracles, teaching and preaching, and enduring persecution.
5. Jesus Christ, the Son of God, was crucified and buried.

6. Christ was raised from the dead and seen of many at different times in various settings.
7. Christ ascended into heaven, sits at God's right hand, and will come again.
8. The Holy Spirit is the third person of the Trinity and teaches us truth, guides us in our walk, gives us gifts, produces fruit in us, and convicts the world of sin.
9. The believer has two natures—the old, which is sinful, and the new, which is righteous.
10. Believers have security, a race course, a prize to win, rewards promised, and a glorious eternity to look forward to.

Can we witness before we understand all these points? Yes. But we may not be prepared for trick questions meant to confuse us. Having this solid foundation is like building on the rock, not on the sand (Luke 6:47–49). When we can proclaim the depth of truth, our voice will be victorious. We may not lead everyone to Christ, but our words will testify of the truth of our Lord Jesus Christ. A sound knowledge will bring assurance to our voice.

Of course, we can witness even if we don't fully understand all these points or are not able to articulate them. But a biblical understanding is necessary for a comprehensive worldview. Eve didn't fully understand God's nature or his purpose, so she was easily fooled by Satan, who appeared as a talking snake. Thus, if we understand the nature and purpose of God, the fullness of the gospel and the Word, and the main points of sound doctrine, we will most likely not be fooled by the enemy, in whatever form he appears to us.

Additionally, our voice is useless if it speaks error. The messages of the false prophets in the Old Testament brought only shame and defeat to Israel. Likewise, if our message fails to exalt Christ, expose sin, and encourage believers, we might as well remain silent. And if it speaks in any tone short of God's love fused with his righteousness and fruit of the Spirit, it doesn't glorify God.

However, if we are firmly grounded in the truth with a full knowledge of the gospel, we will be able to share Christ with a hurting world. We will influence our culture for good, sowing love to drive out hate, shining light to drive out darkness. We will bear spiritual fruit and show real agape love to one another. We will be strengthened for whatever persecution may come. And we will be empowered to live and speak truth, even when the culture demands silence. If we know the truth, we can share it with others and experience victory through voice.

Reflect Further

1. Read Romans 12:2. God's will is good (beneficial), acceptable (advantageous), and perfect (complete). How do we "prove" it to be so?

2. Read Ephesians 4:23 and Colossians 3:10. How does the Holy Spirit and our new nature renew our thoughts, attitudes, and knowledge?

3. Read 2 Peter 3:18. How do we grow in true knowledge when so many errors abound in our culture? Is it really

necessary to study the Word of God? See 2 Timothy
2:15; 3:16–17.

4. In Jude 1:3–4, Jude explains why we must "earnestly con-
tend for the faith" (KJV). Are the conditions and errors he
mentions in verse 4 still present today? How do we combat them?

5. Read Romans 1:16; 1 Corinthians 1:18–31; 2:11–16; and
Colossians 1:10. Do we have all the wisdom we need in
Christ? Is our "growing in knowledge" a matter of learn-
ing more about him—in the Word and in our daily walk?

6. Why would Paul call evangelizing "the foolishness of
preaching" (1 Corinthians 1:21 KJV)? Is he using the term
"foolishness" as what the world thinks of it, though it is really the "wisdom of God" (1 Corinthians 1:21 KJV)? Do we
really have "the mind of Christ" (1 Corinthians 2:16 KJV)?

7. What points of the ancient creeds are specifically covered in 1 Timothy 3:16? Can we infer the other points
from the context and from other Scriptures? What other
Scriptures can you find that list points of the ancient
creeds or of the ten gospel points?

8. Do you believe the Holy Spirit will help you speak the
truth in love, even when the culture demands your silence?

Endnotes

Chapter 2

1. Qtd. in "Justice Scalia: The Tom Wolfe Of Law," by Andrew Geisler, The Federalist online, February 18, 2016, thefederalist.com/2016/02/18/justice-scalia-the-tom-wolfe-of-law/. Accessed January 2, 2021. The quotation has been used as a meme on Facebook and other social media and is a familiar quotation.

Chapter 3

1. Taken from *Post-Christian: A Guide to Contemporary Thought and Culture* by Gene Edward Veith, Jr., © 2020, page 43. Used by permission of Crossway, a publishing ministry of Good News Publishers, Wheaton, IL 60187, www.crossway.org.

Chapter 4

1. *Worldometers.info*, Dover, DE, updated daily, worldometers.info. Accessed February 19, 2021. Also view the page on "Abortions worldwide this year" at worldometers.info/abortions.

Chapter 5

1. This quotation is found in memes on social media and on many famous quote sites. The site *Porridge for the Soul* attributes it to Tozer from *Faith beyond Reason*, © 1989,

2009, https://limpohann.blogspot.com/2014/05/when-does-tolerance-become-compromise.html. Accessed March 21, 2021.

2. "Official Jesus Film Project Ministry Statistics—May 27, 2020," Jesus Film Project, jesusfilm.org/about/learn-more/statistics.html. Accessed January 5, 2021.

3. Ted Baehr, *How to Succeed in Hollywood without Losing Your Soul*, (Washington D.C.: WND Books, 2011), 26-27.

4. Ibid., 27.

5. Ibid.

6. Ibid., 28.

7. Ibid.

8. Ibid.

Chapter 6

1. Many websites attribute this quote to Dietrich Bonhoeffer, though I have found a site that has thoroughly researched his writings and speeches and cannot find that quote. None of the other sites give the reference. In an August 25, 2016 blog, "The Popular Bonhoeffer Quote that Isn't in Bonhoeffer's Works," Warren Throckmorton, a college professor, presents evidence that the quotation is not one that appears in any of Bonhoeffer's writings or recorded speeches. In that blog and in an updated one, he shows evidence that parts of the quote are more correctly attributed to other sources. You may explore his assertions at wthrockmorton.com/2016/08/25/the-popular-bonhoeffer-quote-that-isnt-in-bonhoeffers-works and at wthrockmorton.com/2016/11/11/update-on-a-spurious-bonhoeffer-quote-not-to-speak-is-to-speak-not-to-act-is

-to-act. Accessed March 22, 2021. The readers may come to their own conclusions about this.

Chapter 9

1. Lindy Lowry, "10 Most Dangerous Places for Christians to Live," December 11, 2020, *Open Doors* online, open-doorsusa.org/christian-persecution/stories/dangerous-places-Christians-live. Accessed January 28, 2021.
2. Ibid.
3. Jack Lee, "Persecution: The New Reality for Biblical Christianity in America," *Patheos* online, January 8, 2021, https:www.patheos.com/blogs/chorusinthechaos/persecution-the-new-reality-for-biblical-christianity-in-america. Accessed January 27, 2021. Used by permission.
4. Ibid.
5. Ibid.
6. Ibid.

Chapter 10

1. Christopher F. Rufo, "Critical Race Theory: What It Is and How to Fight It," *Imprimis 50*, no.3 (March 2021): 3. The article is also available online at https://imprimis.hillsdale.edu/critical-race-theory-fight/. Reprinted by permission from *Imprimis*, a publication of Hillsdale College.
2. Ibid.
3. Ibid., 3–4.
4. This statement from "Loving Your Enemies," a sermon by Martin Luther King, Jr., is often quoted in blogs and online posts.
5. *Declaration of Independence*, public domain content. Accessed at Independence Hall Association, Philadelphia,

PA, https://www.ushistory.org/declaration//document/index.html. Accessed May 10, 2021.

6. Ibid.

Chapter 12

1. Grayson Gilbert, "Over Half of the Church Doesn't Believe the Gospel," Blog in online newsletter, *Chorus in the Chaos*, Patheos, August 13, 2020. https://www.patheos.com/blogs/chorusinthechaos/half-church-doesnt-believe-gospel/. Accessed November 11, 2020. Used by permission.

2. Ibid.

3. Ibid.

4. Ibid.

5. Ibid.

6. William D. Watkins, Author, Editor, and President of Literary Solutions, Comment on Facebook post, an informal survey by the author to determine a connection between the lack of gospel understanding and the absence of the study and recitation of ancient creeds. November 11, 2020.

7. Ibid.

8. "Lausanne Covenant: History," Wikipedia, January 5, 2020, https://en.wikipedia.org/wiki/Lausanne_Covenant. Accessed March 23, 2021. Content available under Creative Commons Attribution-ShareAlike License, https://creativecommons.org/licenses/by-sa/3.0/

About the Author

A born-again Christian, Victoria is an ordained pastor who speaks and teaches at local churches and writes Bible studies. She has taught college level composition and literature classes to both traditional and non-traditional students, substituted in several schools, and has worked in both public and private accounting as a former CPA.

In 2020, Victoria published *Victory through Light: How to Overcome the Growing Cultural Darkness*. *Victory through Voice* follows it and continues to expose the cultural decay that threatens our nation. Both books present Christ as the way to overcome the evil in our society. His love, truth, and righteousness are what we must speak to our hurting world.

Victoria has also written award-winning screenplays. In 2012, she published a novel, *Out of the Prison House*, under the pen name of V. D. Carroll, and a collection of literary poetry, *Angel Unaware: Poems*, using the pen name of Victoria Carroll.

Victory through Voice is the second in a planned set of three books to discover and share the power of the True Light—our Lord Jesus Christ. The third book will focus on our spiritual warfare in the midst of the current cancel culture. It will answer several questions, including these: What is our responsibility to our nation, posterity, and fellow Americans? What does God expect us to do in this increasingly immoral nation?

You can learn more about Victoria on her website, where you can subscribe to her blog. You will be able to receive emails with free Bible studies, information about new books as they become available, and news about Victoria's other endeavors. See more at <u>VictoryThroughLight.com</u>.

Dear reader,

If you found this book illuminating and helpful, I invite you to write a review on Amazon.com or another site. It helps me know how I can better serve my readers as I share the light of the gospel of Jesus Christ.

I also welcome you to visit my ministry website, VictoryThrough Light.com. There you can access my blogs and other freebies. You will also find information about my writing and speaking ministry. My hope is that the site will encourage and empower you. You can also visit my author page on Facebook (https://fb.me/VictoriaDorshornAuthor).

My goal is to share the truth that no matter what foe or trial we face, we can be transformed from victim to victor through faith in Jesus Christ. Furthermore, we can confront the growing cultural darkness and overcome its influence on our lives, our relationships, and our society.

We are all commissioned to speak the truth in love, though this is difficult in a culture that increasingly wants us to be silent. Many do not want to hear the message of truth and grace. But we must speak it clearly. And to speak it, we must know it.

Feel free to contact me with questions or feedback. I would love to hear your thoughts about using your voice to speak truth to a dying culture, and, more importantly, how Jesus has helped you deal with increasing persecution for your faith. I love hearing how our Lord Jesus has empowered believers for victorious living. You may email me at vdorshorn@gmail.com.

Also, if you are interested in having me come and speak, please email me at vdorshorn@gmail.com.

In Christ, Victoria Dorshorn

Available through Amazon.com, BarnesandNoble.com,
or other book outlets in print or ebook.

Quantity discounts for your small group or Sunday school class.
Email vdorshorn@gmail.com.

www.ingramcontent.com/pod-product-compliance
Lightning Source LLC
Chambersburg PA
CBHW020254030426
42336CB00010B/753